HISTORY OF THE FUTURE

HISTORY OF THE FUTURE

THE SHAPE OF THE WORLD TO COME IS VISIBLE TODAY

Max Singer

LEXINGTON BOOKS.

Lanham • Boulder • New York • Toronto • Plymouth, UK

Published by Lexington Books
A wholly owned subsidiary of The Rowman & Littlefield Publishing Group, Inc.
4501 Forbes Boulevard, Suite 200, Lanham, Maryland 20706
www.lexingtonbooks.com

Estover Road, Plymouth PL6 7PY, United Kingdom

British Library Cataloguing in Publication Information Available

Library of Congress Cataloging-in-Publication Data
Singer, Max, 1931-
  History of the future : the shape of the world to come is visible today / Max Singer.
       p. cm.
  Includes bibliographical references.
  ISBN 978-0-7391-6486-0 (cloth : alk. paper)—ISBN 978-0-7391-6487-7 (pbk. : alk. paper)—ISBN 978-0-7391-6488-4 (ebook)
  1. International relations—Forecasting. 2. World politics—21st century. I. Title.
  JZ1242.S59 2011
  303.49—dc22

                                                                    2011008579

∞™ The paper used in this publication meets the minimum requirements of American National Standard for Information Sciences—Permanence of Paper for Printed Library Materials, ANSI/NISO Z39.48-1992.

Printed in the United States of America

For Sue

CONTENTS

LIST OF
TABLES AND FIGURES

ACKNOWLEDGMENTS

My first acknowledgment must be to Ben Balint who worked closely with me in developing the structure of the book and who produced many of its words. It is partly his book—except for the faults.

My second debt of gratitude is to my colleagues at the Hudson Institute. This includes both those among whom I first developed much of my thinking years ago in Croton-on-Hudson, and those in Washington where I have had many discussions in recent years. I especially want to mention John Fonte, Hillel Fradkin, Ken Weinstein, and Dianna Furchtgott-Roth. My debt to Herman Kahn is described in a separate note.

I also received valuable help, including in some cases comments on pieces of draft, from Philip Hamburger, Barun Mitra, Premilla and Mohit Satyanand, Harold Rhode, Micha'el Tanchum, David Weil, Nicholas Eberstadt, Daniel Doron, Harold Furchtgott-Roth, and Menachem Milson.

An essential contribution was made by Jack Meinhardt, who edited the whole manuscript before it went to the publisher with great skill and respect for the material. He has been a pleasure to work with—which is not true of all editors. I also had research assistance from several people, including Maoz Brown, Doron Singer, and Avrumy Schreiber.

The book would never have been completed without the help of my wife, Suzanne, who helped me with substance and style and the emotional and practical problems of producing even a short book. My son Saul, who recently published the very successful book about Israeli talent for innovation and entrepreneurship quoted in chapter 4, also provided useful comments.

INTRODUCTION

It is not news that the world is changing—and fast. We all realize clearly how differently our grandparents lived and how different was the world of their grandparents. But how does this change we are experiencing fit into human history, which, after all, has been filled with change?

The story starts by recognizing that until recently for the great mass of people life had remained essentially the same since the Stone Age. During all those millennia people had to spend most of their time producing the food they needed to eat. Our ancient ancestors first lived by using their hands and wits to take food from nature for many thousands of years. But the earth cannot support many hunter-gatherers (or foragers), and the world's population never rose above that of a good-size modern city.

The last big change in how ordinary people lived took place during the long period in which people began to farm and to create the agricultural societies that replaced bands of hunter-gatherers. Farming made it possible for a hundred times as many people to live on the Earth, and for people to live closer together and therefore to build societies large enough and with enough continuity to develop written languages, cities, and advanced culture. In these large societies, small minorities with power were able to take small amounts from many ordinary people and accumulate enough to build high cultures, water systems, roads, cathedrals, and mansions.

But for ordinary people the change from hunting to farming was not clearly a step up. Most farmers had to work harder, and do duller work, than the typical hunter. They had a less varied diet and were generally less healthy and less free.

The change from hunting and gathering to farming changed how ordinary people lived, and made it possible for there to be many more of them, but it didn't do much to improve their living standards, health, or life expectancy. Its most visible effect was to permit the development of a thin upper crust who produced the culture and history that is our patrimony.

All the history we read about, and the cultural glories of millennia of human achievement, are stories of the few. Whether in ancient Greece or the teeming Orient, or during the glorious Renaissance, each special "few" was sustained by masses of people who lived similar lives of toil, squalor, and early death.

Throughout history ordinary people in some societies lived better than ordinary people in other societies, but the difference between best- and worst-off was always relatively small compared to what we see today. The poorest had just enough to feed themselves while the richest, those in the most successful societies, earned perhaps three to four times the cost of a subsistence diet.

Overall there was essentially no economic progress for most people over one hundred thousand years. The best-off early human foragers in the Stone Age lived better than the worst-off peasants at the beginning of the nineteenth century, except that the nineteenth-century peasants could perhaps take some indirect pleasure from the culture available to the rich of their society.

The world's technology had significantly improved during this one hundred thousand years but the main effect was to make it possible for world population to rise to nearly a billion people.

We are now going through a transition that will for the first time decisively change the nature of life for all people—not just a thin upper crust of the rich and the powerful. It will be much quicker than the change from hunting and gathering to farming, and will move us much further away from the conditions that shaped our evolution.

It's not that history is coming to an end but that we are in the middle of switching from one history (or two, if you separate hunter-gathering from agriculture) to a new history. From the time that homo sapiens arose in Africa and began to spread around the world, the vast majority of men and women lived in the old history. Now, however, many have made the transition to a new global history: that of the modern world, which will cover the whole world when the current transition is completed.

There are certain essential characteristics of this new modern world (see Table 1 on page 4), and countries that show all these characteristics have completed the transition to the new history. For example, the "common" people in modern countries live longer, are better educated, and have considerably more wealth, which is produced by a global commercial economy. They tend to live in smaller families, and they have a good deal more political and religious freedom.

One of the biggest ways in which the modern world will be different from the worlds of the past is that in the modern world (when essentially all countries are modern) all people count. That is, describing a modern society requires talking about the great majority of people, not just an upper crust that rides on top of an unchanging mass of poor toilers. Marx and others thought that the effect of industrialization would be to make the mass of workers almost like faceless robots working under the command of a few rich people. But now we can see now that the inherent imperative of modern economies and societies as they get more advanced requires that a greater and greater percentage of workers be able to make choices and be creative. As a result of this imperative, and the changing values and political realities that result, the mass of people influence the direction society takes. In the future, unlike the past, a country can only be changed by changing the ideas or the realities of the mass of citizens.

The world does not change direction like a troop of marching soldiers turning to their flank. The key to understanding the current world is to recognize the way this decisive transition is moving through the world. Some countries, such as England and the United

States, began to change more than a century ago and have already completed their change to modern countries. A few countries, such as Yemen and the Congo, have barely started on the path to becoming modern. The majority of countries are now in the middle of changing from traditional to modern. But we shouldn't be fooled by the difference in timing; all countries are making essentially the same change.

It is an easy mistake to see the current experience of change only as an evolution without end, although it may also be that. The current period is a passage from one kind of world to another. There was change and evolution in the world of the past. There will be change and evolution in the world of the future. But they are fundamentally different worlds, and therefore have different histories. The basic characteristics of human life were the same in all of the different worlds of the past. The new characteristics will shape all of the worlds of the future, however much change lies ahead.

Of course, there will be vast differences—in culture, language, cuisine, and so on—among countries in the long future. But the point of this book is to notice what is common to all. By recognizing the kernel of what is common to every transition from traditional to modern we will understand more of what is happening today and what we can expect from the future. By recognizing the common features of all past worlds, and their contrast with the common features we can expect in all future worlds, we can appreciate the fact that we are in the midst of a unique transition.

This basic perspective about what is happening is the reason we say that countries like the United States, Japan, and Sweden have *completed* their passage to modernity and become modern states. It is not that they have stopped changing. They haven't. But they have passed from one plateau to another. In the future they will change, in unpredictable ways, from one kind of modern country to another. But they will continue to be *modern* countries, and they will continue to be fundamentally different from all traditional countries, in the ways that shall be specified in the following chapters.

One way in which the transition we are going through has made the world today very different from both the past and the future is that now different countries have dramatically different living standards. Some countries are twenty or thirty times as rich as other countries. In the past, and in the future, all countries will have similar living standards. The richest countries will probably again be only three or four times as rich as the poorest.

Since people everywhere have roughly the same qualities of intelligence, strength, and the like, and since basic economic forces tend to produce roughly equal prices for the same products everywhere, the natural condition of the world is for living standards to be roughly the same throughout the world—as they were throughout history. Because the change from traditional to modern ways of living takes each country about a century to complete, and countries started so many years apart, the process of becoming modern has made a world in which the differences among countries are much greater than they were in the past and than they will be in the future. But this current world of great differences between countries is not the world of the future; it is only for the transition period that began in the nineteenth century and will end some two centuries from now.

All countries started the transition almost equal in 1800. Each is beginning its own period of change from traditional poverty to modern wealth at a separate date, and each will complete its passage roughly a century after starting. This picture implies that the inequality between countries must grow during the whole time that many countries are starting on their paths to becoming modern and few have completed the passage. Then, as more and more countries complete the passage to modernity, and fewer and fewer countries remain largely traditional, inequality will begin to diminish. And when all countries have completed the passage, the difference between richest and poorest will again be much smaller.

There are two reasons inequality is beginning to be reduced. The primary and inevitable reason is that countries that are economically behind usually grow faster than the leading countries once they start the process of development, because catching up is easier than breaking new ground. The second, less certain, reason is the tendency for countries that have achieved great wealth to begin to grow more slowly as they begin to value other things more than further wealth, or as they lose the qualities that produced their success.

This book says, "Aha! If all countries are making essentially the same transition from traditional to modern, then we can anticipate the character of the fully modern world by looking at the countries that have already completed their transition, and by looking at the regions of the world that are composed entirely of modern countries." That is why only now—when a significant number of countries have made the transition from traditional to modern—we can tell a partial history of the future.

This leads us to add another big difference between past and future. Fighting and war have always been a central part of human life, but in the future, after all countries have become modern, the war system will disappear. War and the danger of war will no longer be important in people's lives. This seemingly implausible claim is considered in the light of the evidence of what has happened in the main region of the world where all the countries have already become modern, Western Europe. It is not that human nature will be different. People will be as aggressive as ever in the fully modern world. Conflict and power will still be at the center of international relations, but not military power and war.

This view of what is happening—all countries at different times making the same radical change from traditional to modern life—should provide a prism for understanding our current world and recent history. It leads to seeing all the countries that are not yet modern as part of the past; what they do doesn't tell us anything about the future (except for the near future of several centuries during which the transition is being completed). While each country's unique character before it becomes modern will be reflected in its modern character, most of its behavior will be different.

Each child has his or her own special character, but all two-year-olds act more or less like two-year-olds. I am not saying that traditional or transitional countries are infantile. They deserve full respect as unique human communities. But we should expect that the change they are making by becoming modern countries is so profound that it is as mistaken to use their current behavior to predict what they will do after they become modern as it would be to use a child's behavior to predict how he or she will behave as an adult, apart from some elements of personality that persist throughout life.

And just as young children have virtues that they lose when they grow up, traditional countries have virtues that modernization destroys. Modern is not better in all ways, but it is essential to recognize how it is different.

Seeing the world as temporarily populated by countries in different stages of a common transition is a new way of looking at history. When thinking about the long term, it is the most realistic way to look at the world, and it also provides a useful and often ignored perspective for understanding current events.

Can we really be confident that all countries will become modern? Even sub–Saharan Africa? Will modern countries maintain the characteristics that make them modern, or can they backslide or move in different directions? What about the challenge of radical Islam and other ideological movements that are fundamentally opposed to modernization? Can the war system be eliminated without changing human nature or doing away with nation-states? These are questions to be answered in the following chapters.

I

THE KNOWN

1

SHAPING HISTORY BY DEFINING "MODERN"

"Everything's up to date in Kansas City," wrote Oscar Hammerstein, poking fun at country bumpkins who a century earlier had thought they were modern and that earlier generations were backward or traditional.

That is not how "modern" is used in this book. Modernity, here, refers to a new stage in the history of human social development. All modern societies possess a discrete set of interdependent characteristics (see table 1) that makes them modern; a society that has *all* of these characteristics has climbed onto the plateau of the modern world and its history will henceforth be a distinctly modern history. Societies that possess none or some of these characteristics remain, for the time being, in transition from the plateau of the traditional world, where the vast bulk of the population lived essentially as people had for thousands of years.

The current condition of the world, with some countries having made the transition to the modern world while others remain in the traditional world, will not last very long. Within a couple of centuries all countries around the globe will have climbed into the modern world and will have all the characteristics of modern countries. From that point on, all history will be modern.

Prior to about 1800, all societies throughout the world were traditional. In traditional societies, the great majority of people had little

Table 1   Different Worlds

	Traditional	Modern
Life Expectancy	30 years	78 + years
Education (high school)	Practically no one	Almost everyone
Most People Live in	Villages & nomadic bands	Cities
Living Conditions	Dirty, crowded, unpleasant	Comfortable and healthy
Typical Work	Physical, outdoor	Mental or craft
Main Economy	Foraging or subsistence farming	Commercial, international, information dominated
Fertility (in good conditions)	5 to 7 children	Fewer than 3 children
Male-female Relationships	Great role distinction, Male domination	Declining role distinction, Increasing equality
Relationship to Nature	People dominated by nature	People protected from nature; try to protect it
Change & Expectation of Change	Not much	Constant
Choice	Very little	A great deal
Knowledge	Not much	A great deal
Religion	Various, primarily automatic	Various, mostly by choice
Freedom & Self-government	Very rare	Standard

or no education, spent their work time producing food by foraging or subsistence farming, lived in unsanitary hovels in villages or nomadic bands, and worshipped the gods of their parents and forebears.

Culturally speaking, of course, Pharaonic Egypt, Ming China, and Elizabethan England differed greatly from one another. But most of the special features of the world's various cultures were largely the creation and domain of small elites, who were able to go beyond the harsh demands of subsistence work because, one way or another, they had secured arrangements to get some of the output of the large number of ordinary people. In traditional societies around the world, the lives of ordinary people—that is, 70–90 percent of all populations before 1800—were (and are) remarkably alike in the ways listed in the table above. Survival is a harsh mistress.

The big picture is that human history divides into two parts: the old history and the new history. The new history will be written after all countries reach the condition that the most advanced countries reached toward the end of the twentieth century. We are going to learn about that new history by looking at what allowed the advance party, the twenty-odd already-modern countries, to evolve from traditional to modern. From this perspective, everything that happens between these two histories is just a brief transition, which in the long run will be remembered as the era during which the entire world moved from traditional to modern.

It is surprising to realize that, for ordinary people, the change to modern is much bigger than the change from hunter-gathering to farming that began some ten thousand years ago. The left-hand column of table 1.1 describes both traditional farmers *and* their foraging ancestors. A hunter-gatherer could become a subsistence farmer, or a subsistence farmer could become a forager, more easily than either of them could become a Walmart cashier living in a modern city (though Shakespeare or Michelangelo or Aristotle could probably quickly make the necessary adjustments to fit into the modern world). The change to the modern is pervasive, cutting through most aspects of life: how many children we have, where and how we work, our relationships with other people, how we worship, and what we know.

Of course, some features of human life will remain constant. Human nature cannot be expected to change. Our inherent drives and instincts, and the inevitable limits on our capabilities and character, will be the same in the future. Because our behavior is profoundly affected by modern experiences and pressures, however, the unchanging aspects of our nature will manifest themselves in new ways. So this is a story whose end we cannot yet see.

Human diversity will not abate. Most of our traits and capabilities will be distributed unevenly. Both inherent and acquired characteristics—height, beauty, intelligence, strength, sensitivity, and creativity—will be distributed in more or less bell-shaped curves. In the future as in the past, no matter how much we improve ourselves, only half the people will be above average in whatever quality we measure.

Certain essential economic realities will likewise endure. In the future as in the past, most resources will not be unlimited, although as productivity grows most resources except human time will become less scarce. (In the modern era it is people's time, not resources or raw materials, that is most scarce.) As before, higher prices will reduce consumption and increase production, people will be influenced (not always rationally) by patterns of incentives (many of them non-financial), government and private actions will produce unexpected consequences, and most economic actions will yield cascades of indirect effects.

Similarly, with respect to our biological selves, we may live longer in the future, but all people will die. The basic fact of our own mortality will continue to frame our lives, however wealthy and free we become.

For thousands of years, human life has taken shape in societies of tens of thousands or millions of people, and this will continue to be true. Undoubtedly some requirements of mass social living, the inevitabilities of politics, will constrain people of the future as they constrained people of the past. So basic dilemmas of governing will continue to haunt and limit us as we seek to adapt to the new conditions of the future.

Nonetheless, although not everything will change as the world completes its transition from the traditional to the modern, life on the plateau of modern history will be significantly different—not necessarily better, however—for the great masses of ordinary people. Their lives will be governed by different forces and their choices will be made in different contexts. How and where they work will change; their education, relationships, and families will change; their political and religious lives will change. These changes are so sweeping that even the recent past is being rendered increasingly unintelligible in the light of our experience.

BASIC CHARACTERISTICS OF MODERNITY: CONTRASTS AND CONTINUITIES

Throughout history, the overwhelming majority of people lived in dirty, uncomfortable, and often dangerous conditions—a world of poverty, pestilence, and backbreaking labor. They spent all their time providing shelter for themselves and their families, producing food, or bartering with their neighbors. Modern societies, on the other hand, are characterized by unprecedented levels of material prosperity. People get their food and sustenance (and their many forms of entertainment) by working in a complex commercial environment. Very few people grow their own food, make their own clothes, or experience a barter economy. Most people depend on a job working for an institution.

In the past, most economic activity involved using physical resources to produce physical products. In modern exchange economies, by contrast, the most important resource is human capital, that is, the kind of human innovation and operational creativity that increases the potential for ever greater production (by developing new technologies in agronomy and energy, for example). Societies require fewer workers to satisfy their physical needs, and a large and increasing share of products and resources are intangibles, such as coaching, new forms of computer software, business strategies, and relationships.[1] Pre-modern life, to borrow Thomas Hobbes's phrase, was nasty, brutish, and short. The archaeologist Lawrence Keeley examined casualty rates among contemporary hunter-gatherers and found that the likelihood that a man would die at the hands of another man ranged from a high of 60 percent in one tribe to 15 percent in the most peaceful clan.[2] During the twentieth century, in contrast, the chance that a European or American man would be killed by another man was less than one percent. The criminologist Manuel Eisner discovered that homicide rates in Europe had declined by 99 percent from 100 killings per 100,000 people per year in the Middle Ages to less than 1 killing per 100,000 people in modern Europe.[3]

In traditional societies, people were very much in the hands of nature. They suffered when it was cold and faced famine when the rains failed. They often couldn't protect themselves from wild beasts or disease. In the fourteenth century, the bubonic plague, or Black Death, exterminated an estimated 75 to 200 million people. Daniel Bell describes preindustrial life as a "game against nature" in which "one's sense of the world is conditioned by the vicissitudes of the elements—the seasons, the storms, the fertility of the soil, the amount of water, the depth of the mine seams, the droughts and the floods." After industrialization, Bell says, as humans grow less dependent on nature, life becomes a "game between persons" in which people "live more and more outside nature, and less and less with machinery and things; they live with, and encounter only, one another."[4]

Of course, in modern societies some people, such as farmers, have to pay attention to nature, and floods and hurricanes can do much damage, but by and large nature rarely threatens a society's prosperity. (I will discuss global climate change separately in chapter 2.) Instead, people get enjoyment from nature and work to protect the environment. Relieved of the grim struggle for subsistence, modern people live in sanitary and comfortable conditions, protected from the ravages of nature. They work indoors with their minds and their fingers.

In modern life, ordinary people enjoy luxuries unimaginable even to the European aristocrats of ages past. "Louis XIV at the height of his greatness," the French writer Paul Valery writes, "had not the hundredth part of the power over nature . . . which today so many men of low estate enjoy." A majority of people live better today than the most powerful man in Europe 250 years ago. In short, modern man has largely subordinated nature to his own will, just as modern science has reduced much of nature to a set of predictable forces, to "laws of nature" (though we can't be sure that modern science and technology will protect us from all unexpected displays of nature's power, whether volcanic, meteoric, or infectious).

As a result of the taming of nature and advances in medicine, modern people's lives have been dramatically lengthened and physically improved. Before 1800, average life expectancy was less than thirty years, though in the advanced societies of the seventeenth and eighteenth centuries it was somewhat higher. In the modern world, people can expect to live, on average, more than seventy-eight years, 2.5 times as long as in the past. Even if the future adds another forty years to life expectancy, that would not be nearly as big a change as going from thirty to seventy-eight years. In modern life, most people will know their grandparents and their grandchildren, something that was rare in the past. For a woman who bears three or four children, the years devoted to rearing children will be only a fraction of her life.

In the past, almost everyone lived narrow and constrained lives in villages—what Marx called "the idiocy of rural life." In 1800, only 3 percent of the world's population lived in cities. Today, that proportion has already passed the 50 percent mark. In 1920, for the first time in American history, more than half of Americans lived in cities. By 1998, the proportion was 77 percent. In modern societies, most people will live in cities. A villager had little if any regular contact with people outside his village, and likely lived in the same village his entire life. In the future, even if many people choose to live in the countryside or in small communities, their lives will be tied to a much broader part of the world. They will be living what in many ways is "urban life" wherever they live, connected to the larger world by electronic communications systems and high-speed travel.

People in the past were at least as intelligent as people will be in the future. No group of philosophers in the past two thousand years has reached the heights of Socrates, Aristotle, and Plato; no writer has equaled Shakespeare's genius; and no painter has approached Michelangelo's mastery. But people in the past, even the best educated and most informed, knew very little about the physical world, or about other peoples and times. Illiteracy was the norm. In no major society before 1900 did more than a minority of the population enjoy even a basic education, although there have been small societies where the majority was literate. In the modern world, almost all adults attain at least the equivalent of a high school education, and a substantial percentage have higher education. A high school education is important because it affords not only literacy and the possibility of further education, but also a sense of the world's rich variety of peoples and places.

The deepest changes, however, may be the least tangible. Where once there was obedience to authority and submission to power, in modern polities there is political self-government, characterized by the rule of law and the recognition of individual civil rights (such as the right to participate in political power). Whereas uneducated people living in villages tend to think of their status, and the world at large, as unchangeable, modernization instills in men and women the idea of constant change. In the most advanced societies of the past, only some people were free; in modern societies, all people will be free. Most people in past societies—constrained by ignorance, tradition, and social stagnation—had few choices about their lives. Almost all people, for example, felt compelled to accept the religion of their parents or community. Few thought that as individuals they had the power or the right to choose a religion. In modern countries today, most individuals enjoy the freedom to choose their religion, or whether to practice any religion. They also choose where to live, what work to do, and whom, if anyone, to marry. This seems natural and inevitable today, but it was not always so. In modern countries, people's behavior and thinking are much less based on authority—of priests or experts or tradition or the majority.

Modernity is a condition with many attractive features, but also some profound dangers. Becoming modern necessarily means making painful adjustments from life in traditional societies. While most of us usually value being able to make choices, the need to make decisions is also sometimes a burden and a strain, and knowing that we are suffering the consequences not of fate but of our own choices increases the pain. Continuity from one generation to another, while often frustrating, also provides a welcome structure and security to life. Change, the great constant of modern life, makes a great deal of trouble for people, often causing much pain. Modern life puts new demands on people and sacrifices ways of living and relating to each other that were sources of comfort and strength.

SOME OBJECTIONS TO THIS HISTORY OF THE FUTURE

The "invention" of this book is to use a particular definition of "modern" to give shape to history. By naming eras we create new ways of understanding history.

The leading societies have been steadily developing since the industrial revolution began around 1800. They had been changing before then, and they are still changing in unpredictable ways. This book tries to grab history by the throat by determining how advanced a country has to be before it is "modern" and thus permanently fixing the meaning of "modern." I define "modern" as the condition of the most advanced countries in the last part of the twentieth century, and all that they will become after that. I attempt to present the perspective gained by dividing world history into two parts: the past, before 1800, and the future, after all countries reach the point that the most advanced countries reached by the end of the twentieth century.

One might object to this vision of the future by denying that the world is moving from one historical plateau to another. With the onset of the industrial revolution two hundred years ago, this argument goes, the world entered a time of rapid evolution that will continue indefinitely. Each generation will think of itself as modern, but each will be exposed by future generations to be as transitional as all previous generations. There will never be a new plateau of the "modern" from which we can view the past and look back on the period of transition from traditional to modern.

Since we cannot predict the future with any precision, it is hard to refute this argument. Undoubtedly, the future will offer new and unexpected forms of technology, communication, music, architecture, and so on. These innovations will alter human life in unpredictable ways, changing who we are and how we think. But the basic features of the modern will likely remain in place, judging from the evidence available today. All modern countries possess all fourteen characteristics listed in table 1. As countries acquire the fourteen characteristics, they become modern and begin behaving like already-modern countries. It seems likely that modern countries will continue to exhibit these characteristics.

A second objection says that the history of the future began earlier than we place it. According to this view, the industrial societies of the early twentieth century, with their vast increases in wealth and population, were fully modernized and part of the future, not just part of the transition. Shouldn't we regard World War I, for example, as a war between modern countries, at least on the Western Front, clearly different from all earlier wars? The brief answer is that the continued evolution in advanced countries during the twentieth century was too significant to ignore. "Post-industrial" information-dominated economies are significantly different in their demands on people from earlier phases of the transition when mass manufacturing was the center of the economy.[5] I only include the former among the twenty-odd modern countries, and these countries hadn't yet completed their passage to modernity fifty or a hundred years ago.

A third objection is that it is premature to speak of the end of one kind of history (traditional) and the beginning of a new kind of history (modern). Some will argue that a century from now it may become clear that even the most advanced countries today do not possess truly modern characteristics—in terms, perhaps, of world government, the extension of human life, and the end of income growth in the most advanced countries. This objection doesn't deny the fundamental division between the worlds of past and future; it just says that even the most advanced countries today are still in transition to the world of the true future. We are too self-congratulatory when we assert that we have already achieved true "modernity."

Again, the test I use to check whether we can recognize when the history of the future has begun is the list of characteristics of the modern world. If another century produces a new set of characteristics, as different from our list of the characteristics of the modern world as our list is from the characteristics of the traditional world, then we are guilty as charged of generational presumption. But it is not easy to imagine such a new set of characteristics.

It should be said that the list of fourteen characteristics has some arbitrariness. Why is modern life expectancy defined as seventy-eight years, not seventy-five, or seventy-seven, or eighty? I chose seventy-eight because all countries that fit the definition of modern, and only those countries, have life expectancies of seventy-eight. Obviously there is no significant difference between a life expectancy of seventy-eight, seventy-seven, or seventy-six. The actual number is just a means of defining a border that is inherently ambiguous. And life expectancy is continuing to rise in all countries. The real distinction is between life expectancy in modern countries (now seventy-eight) and life expectancy in countries that are less advanced.

It is also true that many of the characteristics used to define modern countries also apply to slightly less advanced countries. ("Advanced" means "later" not "better.") Roughly speaking, less advanced industrial economies are more likely to be dominated by manufacturing industries that mass-produce physical goods. Modern economies are dominated by service industries and the production of intangible goods and services. Less modern economies are more concerned with things, while the most modern economies revolve around information. Of course, modern economies, too, often have agriculture, extractive industries, and manufacturing industries, and the major post-industrial categories of service and information industries are quite different and diverse. Haircuts are a service, but scarcely postindustrial. Much work of the information industries is used in support of the production of hard things like cars, as well as "hard" services like electricity. So broad categories have only limited meaning.

What matters is the nature of the work people are doing. People working on the assembly-line of a large, old-fashioned factory will respond to the world differently from people making calculations in an office. As a society becomes more advanced not only does the amount of work involving physical strength and physically stressful working conditions decline, but the amount of work requiring individual judgment, human interaction, and creativity increases. This is partly because people's time becomes more valuable so that it becomes worthwhile to avoid using people for work that doesn't demand human qualities. In a modern economy, the majority of people are doing such work. In addition, the greater complexity and interdependence in more advanced economies provides more opportunities for individuals to get ahead by finding some "new angle" for producing or profiting, either a new specialization or a new coordination required by others' specializations. Therefore, a significant number of people, not just executives and major entrepreneurs, are engaged in genuinely creative, autonomous efforts, usually involving learning from and influencing other people. This is already true for many people long before societies become "post-industrial." So for many purposes it is reasonable to use a less stringent test and to think of more than the twenty-odd most advanced countries as "modern." The predictions here about how much of the world will be modern by the end of this century probably depend on such a more generous definition of modern.

A keen appreciation of the importance of the difference between the most advanced countries of the middle of the twentieth century and those same countries by the end of the century comes from reading Aldous Huxley's view of the future in *Brave New World*, written in 1932. The God of Huxley's feared future world was Henry Ford, because Huxley thought the future would be dominated by assembly lines, with people becoming more and more like automatons. He understood his time but was wrong about the direction of the future. In today's advanced countries, the direction is clearly toward more individuality and creativity in work, just the opposite of Huxley's vision. The assembly line is the icon of a stage that modern countries have passed through, not the paradigm for the future. That is why I do not call the countries of Huxley's time "modern." They were on the way but they hadn't yet arrived.

Since our experience so far is that all industrial countries continue their economic and social development until their economies become post-industrial, the question of where to draw the line doesn't matter much. Many of the features of modern life, including most of its physical features, came earlier, when the modern countries still had primarily industrial economies. The softness of the distinction is unavoidable and matters little because all countries have passed or will pass through the grey area, which makes it harder to keep score, but doesn't affect the final result.

THE NATURE OF THE MODERN

"Modern" refers to the specific constellation of fourteen conditions listed in table 1 that, once attained, continue into the indefinite future. Thus modernization is not merely industrialization, or rising incomes, or the growth of gross national product, or technological progress. Taken individually, each of these indicators leaves out essential dimensions of human development. "Modern" is a package of characteristics, which, once set in motion, does not rest until all the characteristics have been achieved. Together, they form a coherent set of social, cultural, and political changes. A country that stubbornly resists change in one area will likely be underdeveloped in the others. Countries that resist democratization—for instance, Cuba, Myanmar, and North Korea—are also weak in economic growth and education levels. A country that succeeds in attaining at least some features of modernity, by contrast, will eventually succeed in attaining the others. So by "modern" we mean the total condition of a society that makes it fundamentally different from traditional societies. When a country has made all those changes it has become a modern country.

What if a country has three or eleven characteristics of a modern country? Such a state, I believe, is possible only temporarily. All the characteristics of modernity go hand in hand; they cause and reinforce each other. No one doubts, for example, that such physical characteristics as long life and healthy living conditions are bound together. But some form of democracy, some freedom of religion, and substantial sexual equality are also inevitable characteristics of a modern world.

Modernizing involves constant interaction between changes in the way people work and the other changes in education, institutions, and attitudes that result from, and are necessary to create, more efficient ways of working. These changes are qualitative, like the difference between a horse-drawn wagon and a car, not differences of degree. For some of the changes between traditional and modern—such as differences between village and city life, or differences in the kinds of work people do or the nature of the economy—the stark, qualitative nature of the difference is plain to see. But this is true of the less obvious changes as well. A world in which people routinely live to ninety, for example, would not be drastically different from a world in which they live to seventy-eight. But life is very different in traditional societies, in which most people die before the age of thirty (though, on average, those who don't die as infants or small children live well past thirty). Similarly, education levels may well keep rising steadily, but the real change is from traditional widespread ignorance to the levels of education and knowledge typically available to all citizens of modern countries.

Since modernity is a fixed target, not a relative ranking, once a country is modern it stays modern; it doesn't go on to be "very modern" or "super modern." There are only two kinds of countries: modern and not-yet modern. Modern countries can keep getting richer, and so far most of them have, but they do not become "more modern." There is a threshold, a discrete set of conditions of life, that separates all modern countries from all other countries. Once the world is modern, it will stay modern until something happens that changes the character of human life as much as it was changed by the passage from the conditions of the past to modern conditions. If life expectancy were to change not by thirty or forty years but by five hundred years, for example, that might imply a new kind of future on another "plateau." But simply getting richer or moving faster or doing more modern miracles with our cell phones (even if they are implanted in our ears and completely wireless) would not be enough to change the character of human life as much as the change from traditional societies to modern countries.

Certainly some countries are closer than other countries to becoming modern. Mexico and Brazil are now significantly different from Nigeria and Bangladesh. None of them is modern, but Mexico and Brazil are more nearly modern, and this difference affects how they behave. Even though they cannot yet be reliably expected to behave like modern countries, nearly modern countries act more and more like modern countries as they come closer to becoming modern themselves, and as the examples of modernity become more powerful.

Many modern ideas, and many features of modern life, have appeared in different places and at different times in history, but always as isolated fragments that affected only a fraction of the population. There was democracy in some ancient Greek cities, although not for the whole population. Modern rejection of authority and modern ideas became important in intellectual circles by at least the eighteenth century, and less widely even earlier. But never have there been whole countries at all comparable to today's modern countries. When a whole country acquires all the characteristics of modernity, it becomes something different, a new kind of organism with its own structure and dynamics. You can't learn about that from looking at isolated elements of what could be called "modernity" in the past. These elements of modernity only have their full effect when combined as they are in modern countries, then in regions, and finally in the entire world.

Nor can we tell what modern countries are like from the behavior of the "most modern" countries of the past, say Germany in 1914 or 1930. The most modern countries of the past may have been on the way to becoming modern, but they had not yet changed enough to acquire the characteristics that define fully modern countries.

During the next century or so all countries will become modern. That is, all countries will acquire the characteristics that modern countries have now. (And the modern countries will continue to have those characteristics.) The basic features of modern life—health, comfort, and freedom—are so attractive to people, and each step of increased productivity necessary to gain modern life can be made in so many ways and so easily, that the modernization process is essentially impossible to stop. Countries can stop their own modernization for a while, accidentally or on purpose, but it will continue in other countries, and eventually restart wherever it is stopped.

Of course, nothing is really inevitable. The earth could be struck by a meteorite tomorrow and all human life destroyed. A new religion that rejects private property and economic development could sweep the world, converting everybody to its precepts. But it would take such an unlikely never-before-experienced development to stop the modernization process.

Many have observed that the world today is starkly divided. As Oxford professor, Amartya Sen put it, "we live in a world of unprecedented opulence, of a kind that would have been hard even to imagine a century or two ago . . . And yet we also live in a world with remarkable deprivation, destitution and oppression."[6] The simple reason for this jarring anomaly is that the world now is a mix of past and future. For any given nation, this passage from tradition to modernity usually takes something more than a century.

The Nobel Prize–winning economist Robert Lucas, Jr., has made a mathematical model that reasonably accurately describes the last two centuries of world economic history by using the analogy that in 1800 each country in the world was lined up on a track behind a starting gate. Each country's gate opened at a different time. The first was England, early in the nineteenth century. Since then most countries' gates have opened and they have each started on the same kind of path that no one had ever gone down before. Many countries have already followed the path far enough to become what I call modern countries, but there are still a few countries whose gates have not yet opened.

One point of Lucas's model, and of the view of the world described here, is that the whole experience of the world can be seen as a single process and a single path, even though countries start at different times and each has its own version of the common path. The complicated and confused state of the world that we see is the result of the patterns that develop from the different timings.

Lucas also points out that the economic history of the last two hundred years is consistent with the simple generalization that countries that start later, and are behind, grow faster than the leading countries. This process initially results in great gaps between the richest and poorest countries, as some countries get out of the gates earlier than others. Before 1800, for example, the richest countries were only three or four times richer (for the average person) than the poorest countries, or even than Stone Age bands. By 2000, however, the richest countries were nearly thirty times richer than the poorest. Lucas shows that a continuation of the same process—with the countries that started on the path later growing faster than those that are far ahead—will over the next two centuries gradually restore the pattern of nearly equal wealth between countries, but at a much higher, modern level.[7]

To try to understand the future by looking at a static snapshot of the world today is as misleading as looking at a family portrait and assuming that the aging grandfather and the young granddaughter will be that way permanently. In the snapshot, for example, Italy looks today very different from Bangladesh. But in a longer view, both Italy and Bangladesh can be seen as countries that started in the same condition and that fairly soon will again be in the same condition. Both used to be traditional countries, in which most people were subsistence farmers living in villages. Italy started on the new path of increasing productivity nearly a century ago and has now crossed over to the world of the future. Bangladesh only recently began to follow the same path and won't join Italy for a century or so. In the long view, then, Italy and Bangladesh appear as similar countries at different points along a common path. Of course, when both Italy and Bangladesh are equally modern countries, they will be different from each other, just as they were different from each other when they were both traditional countries.

The fact that all of the countries in the world are (or will be) traveling along the same path does not mean that the final destination is global culture. Cultural heritages are remarkably resilient. A society's heritage—whether shaped by Protestantism, Catholicism, Islam, Confucianism, communism, Frenchness, or Anglo-Saxon values—leaves a lasting imprint on its worldview. Although the process of industrialization began in the West, modernization is not Westernization. It is an "infection" that hit the West first, beginning two centuries ago, but will hit the whole world before it is through. East Asia, after all, has had the world's highest economic growth rates, and India is now sustaining economic growth rates of about eight percent a year. The transformation we are witnessing is the result of an inexorable process that can be expected to change the whole world in the same way, probably before the end of the next century. (One exception to this schedule may be sub–Saharan Africa, which I discuss in chapter 2.)

Because modernization has been working for some two centuries, a full understanding of the dynamics of that history can disclose a great deal about how the process will continue to work through the part of the world that is not yet modern. Although the future is vast and unknowable, we can know some of its broadest outlines. Without engaging in prophesy, we can attain a realistic vision of the future path of most of the nations of the world, not because nations have development, decay, and death written in their genes, but because we can see what modernization will do to nations by looking at what it has done to those that were first to feel its effects. We can, by analogy, foresee what will happen to first-graders by knowing what has become of past first-graders. Of course, the paths of nations are less humanly familiar, and offer an incomparably smaller sample. Predicting the precise path of any given country would be as foolish as predicting the life story of any one of the first-graders. Yet you can reach a realistic sense of the life of the group even though you know almost nothing of what will happen to each individual.

The modernization process is what happens in countries as they learn to be more productive and thus steadily increase the amount they produce each year. In order to achieve increased productivity, a society has to change economically, socially, and politically. And the wealth produced by growing productivity also changes the society. While most people focus on the *effects* of increased wealth, it is quite possible that these effects are not as important as the effects of the changes needed *to produce* the wealth. That is why countries do not become modern if their wealth comes from oil or something else that the society does not produce.

The idea that within the next couple of centuries the entire world (or most of it) will be wealthy and free is not entirely optimistic. Certainly there is much about modern life that one can regret or dislike. It will make new problems for people, as discussed in the epilogue. In the end it may be a disaster. People might well be less happy or less good in the modern world. And we may find a way to destroy ourselves. Rather than acting as an advocate for modernity (it doesn't really need an advocate, as it is coming whether we like it or not), I simply hope to describe the basic features we can expect in the modern world. If people understand these basic features, they will be better able to change what can be changed, which is most things, and make the best of modern life.

Nor is the expectation improbable. Past experience suggests that the estimate that the world will become modern within the next two centuries is conservative. Although there are significant barriers to future modernization that didn't stand in the way of past modernization, there were also significant barriers in the past that are now gone or have become much weaker.

AN IMPORTANT ELEMENT OF OPTIMISM

Once significant regions of the world have completed their passage into modernity, a new and unexpected feature of modernity will appear.

Modern countries have the fourteen characteristics shown in table 1. When all the countries in a region are modern, that region gains a fifteenth characteristic: It no longer has the war system that has existed since states began. That is, the nature of international relations within the region changes. This has already happened in Western Europe, which (like North America) has become what we call a "Zone of Peace," a region within which the war system has disappeared.[8]

When all the countries in the world have become modern countries, the whole world will become a Zone of Peace and the war system will have disappeared from the planet (though this does not guarantee that there will be no wars).

Chapter 4 describes the practical reasons that the inherent characteristics of modern countries—without any need for people or political systems to become wiser or more moral—will lead to the end of the war system when all countries are modern countries. Although war is an ancient human activity, and has produced much value in human life, the end of the war system will be a great benefit for humanity.

While the picture of the future I have begun to set forth in this chapter—a vision of worldwide affluence, robust economic growth, physical comfort, rising educational levels, rising life expectancy, freedom of choice, and democratic governance throughout the whole world—may surprise, even startle, some readers, this line of reasoning is hardly radical. Even though the picture is composed of statements about the future, the method of the book is simply an exercise in understanding and applying history, in deducing what hasn't happened yet from what has happened already. As Dante writes in the Inferno: "You may understand, therefore, that all our knowledge shall be a dead thing from that moment on / when the door of the future is shut." Close the door of the future, and our present knowledge becomes sterile.

Throughout the past, history was generally seen as either cyclic or as a decline from a past golden age. By discerning the driving force that has changed the world in recent centuries, however, we can view the modernization that has been the dominant feature of recent history as the result of a recognizable process that, beginning in the nineteenth century, acquired a life of its own while spreading through the world. Fortunately, in tracing modernization's path into the future, we have a fund of historical experience to draw upon.

The modernization process is infinitely complicated and is influenced by many centuries of history in different parts of the world. I will not describe much of this historic process. My argument is that somehow something new and very powerful gradually started in some places in the nineteenth century—sustained growth in per capita national production—and that this basically new process, whatever its roots, has been making more and more countries into modern countries, and will continue until it has made all countries modern.

NOTES

1. Yuval Levin, "Recovering the Case for Capitalism," *National Affairs* (Spring, 2010).

2. Lawrence Keeley, *War before Civilization: The Myth of the Peaceful Savage* (New York: Oxford University, 1996).

3. Manuel Eisner, "Modernization, Self-Control and Lethal Violence: The Long-Term Dynamics of European Homicide Rates in Theoretical Perspective," *British Journal of Criminology* (2001) 41:618-632.

4. Daniel Bell, *The Coming of Post-Industrial Society: A Venture in Social Forecasting* (New York: Basic Books, 1973).

5. The strongest academic body of evidence about the behavior of modern countries, the work of Ronald Inglehart and others based on many years of international surveys of people's values, shows clearly both the change in people's values as countries become industrial (from pre-industrial) and a further distinct change in values as countries move from industrial to post-industrial—that is, to "modern" as I define it (Ronald Inglehart and Christian Welzel, *Modernization, Cultural Change, and Democracy: The Human Development Sequence* [New York: Cambridge University Press, 2005]).

6. Amartya Sen, *Development as Freedom* (New York: Knopf, 1999).

7. Robert E. Lucas, Jr., *Lectures on Economic Growth* (Harvard University Press, 2002), p. 97.

8. See Max Singer and Aaron Wildavsky, *The REAL World Order: Zones of Peace; Zones of Turmoil* (Chatham, NJ: Chatham House, 1993).

2

WHERE DOES WEALTH COME FROM AND WHY IS IT SPREADING?

Poverty is the natural condition of human beings. It is only by learning how to create wealth on a massive scale that an increasing number of humans have recently been able to escape poverty.

Before 1800 people in many societies learned how to become better producers, but in all cases the effect of the increase in wealth was to elevate a thin upper crust and increase population faster than the ability to increase output, so the living standards of ordinary people never rose much. This was the Malthusian trap in which the world lived until recently.

But at the beginning of the nineteenth century something new began to happen. England began to steadily increase its productivity and its wealth at the same time as its population began to grow rapidly. Both continued over many years. Wealth grew faster than the population, and the increased number of people had more wealth and better living conditions. Somehow the world began to escape from the age-old Malthusian trap, only a short time after Malthus described it.

Between 1820 and 1973 England grew from twenty-one million to fifty-six million people and English average real income grew from $1,700 to $12,000 (in 1990 dollars). Shortly after England began this new process of simultaneous economic and population growth, the process spread to other countries in Western Europe and to the United States. Later it began spreading to other parts of the world.

There is much controversy among economists and historians about why this process of economic development began when and where it did, and why it is spreading unevenly, country by country, with long delays between countries. We have enough experience with the process of economic growth, however, to draw some practical conclusions about where we can expect this process to go in the future, much as we can know what happens to a car when the driver presses the accelerator, even if we don't understand the workings of the internal combustion engine.

DEVELOPMENT AS "NATIONAL LEARNING"

Modernization is essentially a national learning experience. Partly this is a matter of individuals learning how to be more skilled and efficient. More importantly, as a country develops, it adds layer upon layer of new strengths that can be used by its workers. While some of these new strengths are improvements by the government, most are capabilities of individuals, companies, and other organizations that are useful to people operating in an advanced way but not practical at earlier stages of development.

A peculiar relationship exists between workers and their country. It is the individual worker who becomes more productive, but the amount of value an individual can produce depends on the national culture and economy as well as on the worker's own efforts. If a senior American executive who earns (produces) half a million dollars a year moves to India, she will almost certainly not be able to earn more than a fraction as much. Indians are not less productive than modern Americans because they are somehow inferior. There are many men and women in India who are as productive as the many highly productive Indians working on Wall Street and in Silicon Valley. Most Indians cannot yet be highly productive in India, however, because India is still in the process of *learning* how to be a modern society. It is still developing all the facilities and connections and laws and regulations needed to make the highest productivity possible. India has not yet become a modern country, though in some areas—such as call centers and some medical tourism—it may be as advanced as any country.

Workers cannot be as productive in a country that has not yet learned to be modern because high productivity depends on specialization of work, and one cannot fully specialize if all the other specialties are not available to do their parts of the job. A worker cannot be highly productive as an ace designer of corporate communication systems in a country in which few corporations use special communication systems, or there aren't enough people qualified to help implement clever new systems. An advanced economy is immensely complicated because it has gradually increased efficiency by higher specialization, which it accomplishes by gradually developing what each specialty needs, along with all the required links to bring the specialties together efficiently. The development of that complexity, and everything needed to support it, is what I call a national learning experience.

This is the reason a country cannot leap into the modern world but must go through the development process step by step. A Chinese or Indian company cannot just copy a company in the United States or Japan, even if it buys all the same equipment and imports the same managers, because the working environment in China and India is different and cannot provide what is found in more advanced countries (though it may offer certain advantages, even apart from lower costs).

What determines how fast a country increases its productivity and wealth is how amenable its people, organizations, and institutions are to change. Growth requires change and change always involves pain, dislocation, and doubt. There is no rule about how fast a country should change. Faster may or may not be better. But no one makes the decision. The speed of modernization is determined by millions of actions and choices by people, in their own lives and in their community, who cannot know how their choices affect the overall result, as well as by the government and political system. It is the net effect of all these choices that constitutes the national "decision" about how fast to increase national productivity and wealth.

National learning, as a country improves its social, political, and business environment, resembles individual learning in that some countries learn more quickly than others. Obviously, some cultures make learning easier and some make it harder. But cultures can gradually be modified to become more amenable to the necessary learning. Everyone can learn.

The notion of national learning supplies a key to thinking about how countries become wealthy. But it is a metaphor. A country doesn't have a mind that learns. Individual citizens have to learn and change. Most of the drive toward increased productivity comes from individuals seeking ways to improve their lives by being more efficient, either by producing more or better products or by bringing together those who produce and those who consume (that is, marketing).

While there are many difficult questions about economic development, the bottom line for anyone who wants to know whether to expect the currently poor countries to become wealthy is clear—and not controversial, at least among economists who study the issue. When a few key internal barriers are lifted, every country can be expected to grow until it, too, becomes modern. The most important fact about recent economic history is this: No country that has accomplished the few "simple" things required for growth is failing to grow about as fast as the United States and England grew as they moved from traditional to modern countries, and most are growing faster.

PREREQUISITES FOR ECONOMIC DEVELOPMENT

Modernization requires minimum adequate government. Any country will gradually make itself more productive if it has a government that enforces a rule of law that protects property rights, enforces contracts, and provides for internal peace and a reasonably stable currency.

In advanced countries, there are many disputes about what "property rights" include and exactly how much respect the legislature must give them. For countries starting to develop, however, these refined issues are not yet important. "Property rights" exist when ordinary people understand that powerful people, or the government, cannot take their property away from them—that an independent judiciary and a reasonable police force operate to protect them from bandits and politicians, enabling them to keep what they produce. The protection of property rights also requires a land registration system that provides a clear and enforceable title to land so that it can be sold and mortgaged.

"Contract rights" exist when people believe that if they make a business agreement they can usually have confidence that the other party will do what is promised because that is the way the country works, and because there is a good chance that if necessary a court will compel the other party to perform.

Contract and property rights do not have to be perfect in order to be sufficient to enable productivity to begin to grow. In fact, no country provides perfect protection, and some issues depend on controversial questions of value and policy. The basic need is for rights to be protected enough so that most people find it prudent to work to increase what they have by becoming more productive rather than by seeking power.

For many countries, it is not easy to achieve minimum adequate government. Some, especially in sub–Saharan Africa, seem endlessly mired in internal conflict and dominated by corruption and exploitative rulers. The good news is that all significant studies show that no country faces serious obstacles to the economic part of the task if it overcomes the political difficulties. In today's world, economic growth is easy and natural. Neither well-organized administrative systems nor advanced economic analysis is needed to get a country started. Where economic growth is missing, government is likely standing in the way or failing its minimal responsibilities.

The fundamental fact about traditional economies is that an individual's time has little value. In traditional societies, most laborers—however smart, creative, and energetic—do not produce much value. Because they cannot earn much income from selling their time, they instead spend their time making things for their own consumption. People work hard to obtain food, but do little additional labor; even though they have practically nothing—no fancy clothes, barely adequate shelter, few comforts or amusements—the little they could add by working more doesn't seem worth the effort.

The transition to modern economies began when, one country at a time, people learned how to achieve sustained increases in productivity, cumulating year after year and producing the unprecedented wealth now evident in countries like the United States and Japan. In 2003 American workers produced thirty times as much value per hour worked as American workers did in 1820. Japanese workers in 2003 produced fifty times as much per hour as Japanese workers did in 1870, a much faster rise from a lower base.[1]

Where does this productivity come from? Clearly modern workers are not trying thirty or fifty times harder, and they are not thirty or fifty times smarter, though they do have ten times as many years of schooling.

Probably the most fundamental cause is that work is continually being divided more efficiently, with more and more specialization. Or to say it another way, more and more people are unintentionally cooperating with each other. Specialization, as we have seen, is an essential part of the national learning process; it is happening within countries, and increasingly it is happening on a global basis.

The first stages of specialization are easy to appreciate. Obviously, it is more efficient for some people to cut trees and produce lumber while other people make furniture. But modern economies are far beyond that. Now we are at a point where generally no one makes anything; each person knows how to do one or two tiny parts of the job of producing a finished product, such as a computer mouse. Few people know how to produce something from the raw materials, and only a small fraction of workers are making physical things. Partly this is because the main output is services rather than goods. In advanced economies, most of the workers who produce things like cars or telephones are not actually cutting steel or assembling microphones; rather, they are designing, selling, planning, keeping records, organizing, and doing other "intellectual" tasks to provide the services needed in connection with the physical production process.

The result, in advanced economies, is an infinitely more complex and constantly shifting and adjusting production process. The economy's efficiency depends on the whole system, in which consumption and production are woven together. The function of coordinating everyone's independent efforts is so important that the country can afford an unfathomable process (the free market) to do the job, even though the process involves a lot of people making a living doing things that don't seem at all productive, and some people making absurd amounts of money. Nature avoids many decisions by creating millions of seeds for each plant that grows and "wasting" all the other seeds it produces. We make decisions through a system that generally judges value on the basis of what a free buyer is willing to pay, and which allows millions of people to make money by finding some way to do something—however useless it seems—that someone is willing to pay for, because any other system produces worse results.

The driving force of modernization is as powerful as it is simple: the human desire to better one's lot through initiative and creativity. Sometimes this happens in dramatic steps: An investor opens a new business that can afford to employ many people at higher salaries than they made before. A particularly dramatic example is Edwin Land's invention of instant pictures, and the creation of the Polaroid Company, which became a major corporation but then was made obsolete by new technology that provided a better way to produce the benefits Polaroid had been selling. More often, increased production happens in incremental improvements: A farmer starts using a better fertilizer and is able to grow more than before; a villager rents his cell phone to neighbors who can't afford their own; a mail clerk in a large company figures out and implements a way to stack more boxes in the same space. For Indian farms, to take a real-world example, simple innovations could reduce storage losses from the 25 percent level common in rural parts of India to the 3 percent suffered in modern areas. Some improvements are "pushed" by someone who is selling something needed to make the improvement. Others are "pulled" by someone who sees an opportunity and looks for what is necessary to make it work.

There are an infinite number of ways to increase productivity. All of them, however, begin with the imperative to change. The craftsman finds that he can't earn enough money selling his chairs unless he is able to assemble more chairs by buying partly finished pieces of wood to shape and put together. Factory workers have to accept new tools and new ways of organizing their work. Office workers who have grown complacent with a way of working that had always been successful find they are under pressure to work differently, often in ways they initially resist. If people think they are doing about as well as can be expected, there may be little pressure for change. But if people see that others, not unlike themselves, are doing better, they become motivated to look for ways to do better themselves. One key to spurring invention or improvement is learning that someone else has been able to do something that you haven't yet been able to do.

This increase in productivity is accompanied by far-reaching social changes—like urbanization. As laborers' time becomes more valuable, and as they move from static lives in villages to places like city slums, they often work more hours. Workers are pushed away from the farms, because fewer people are needed to grow more crops on the same land, and pulled to cities because there are more ways to become more productive in cities. They are attracted even by urban slums, not only by the possibility of earning more money but by the excitement and vitality cities afford. Indeed, one sign of the strength of people's desire to better themselves is the massive worldwide migration to cities. They take grave risks and accept the pain of changing their lives because they think they can earn more— that is, be more productive—in the city, and mostly they turn out to be right. The slums stay horrible, but many people move through them and out into better lives in the growing city.

The modernizing world affords many opportunities to increase productivity. Each time a worker seizes an opportunity to improve his condition, productivity goes up. One of the reasons there are always and everywhere opportunities to increase productivity in the modernizing world is that the technical possibilities and the patterns of prices around the world are always changing. Every change opens new opportunities to increase productivity. An increase in salaries for some kind of work in the United States, for example, may create new opportunities to outsource that work to India, where qualified people will work for less.

CAN THE GROWTH OF PRODUCTIVITY BE STOPPED?

There will always be some workers too risk averse to make changes, too unimaginative to seize possibilities, or too dominated by habit to break away from the past. But even if the vast majority proves too weak to initiate change, others will take the initiative. Most will take only small steps, or take only opportunities that are handed to them in small bites, but a bold few will pursue bigger changes. If there is no one in a village or community who is ready to pursue opportunities, others from outside will bring the opportunities in because they can profit from producing and marketing new products or recruiting workers.

The people of India offer one of the most dramatic examples of this phenomenon. When this century dawned, half of India's population consisted of villagers who grew their own food and were largely cut off from their country's growing commercial sector. Many villages had no roads that trucks could use to bring supplies or to pick up harvests, if there had been commercial crops to transport. Now Mumbai and Bangalore are home to some of the most sophisticated businesses in the world, though only a few miles away life in the countryside has changed little for centuries.

Low prices for land and labor in Indian villages represent opportunity for those who have made money in the cities. Already, private schools for peasants' children are flourishing in poor villages where government schools represent something closer to political payoffs than public services. Indians are learning to read and write and to use their political power to force the government to begin to do its job. Mobile phones have spread even to backward villages. As more money is available in the villages, and as other tools become as affordable as mobile phones, such villages will become important markets and connections will form between the village population and the modern economy. Some people will leave the villages for cities, while others will find ways to make money where they are—by improving their farming, by bringing tools or consumer items into their village to sell, or by creating services for the locals from the national sector. Eventually, local political power will force the government to build roads. A whole new set of opportunities will then arise to service the commercial trucks and others using the road. The road will change the economics of everything in the village and strengthen the connection between the village and the rest of the country. Anything that happens to change the cost of goods in the village creates new opportunities to do what had been uneconomic before. Here, as elsewhere, change creates new possibilities for improvement.

Change, however, can be difficult. Along with the kinds of sweeping changes associated with modernization come much dislocation and alienation, as families are divided and communities disrupted. Some people insist that modern life and higher incomes aren't universally attractive. Modern ways often are perceived as corrupt, immoral, or decadent. Undoubtedly, in many countries there will be some who choose to resist modernity.

Is it possible that wealth will not spread to some countries because their citizens choose to avoid the evils associated with modernization? Experience strongly suggests that no country as a whole will permanently make that choice. It is difficult to imagine that any country would choose to remain traditional and poor for generations while watching other similar societies become free, urban, and wealthy. (The case of Islam will be discussed separately in chapter 5.) Those countries that insist on practices that are incompatible with economic modernization—as with the Soviet Union last century—will sooner or later find themselves lagging behind and marginalized. The holdouts against modernity in every country will eventually give in to the siren song of modernity's appeal.

Are the advantages of modernity worth the price? People can and will debate this question, but the fact is that modernity is not a choice. It is coming whether we like it or not, whether the price is too high or not. People in particular countries can slow or stop their own economic growth, usually when they fail to recognize the effect of what they do. But the pressure of people's desire to improve their lives, combined with the power of example in countries that are getting ahead, will eventually pull all countries along the path until they reach modernity. One of our challenges now is to minimize the costs of modernization as we become familiar with the negative features of modern societies and find ways to reduce or adjust to them.

GOVERNMENT OBSTACLES TO INCREASED PRODUCTION

Wherever adequate minimum government exists, economic growth is natural. In a country in which productivity fails to grow, we shouldn't ask what the government is failing to do; rather, we should look for how it is preventing people from increasing productivity.

Governments can inhibit growth by making political power a safer route to success than economic productivity. If young people, especially, believe that they risk losing the fruits of success to those with political power, or to strong-arm tactics backed by political power, or if they see that they can more easily get ahead by seeking political power, then much of the country's productive potential will be lost. One measure of excessive political rapacity is capital flight. If most people who are able to acquire capital move it out of the country because they think it is more productive or safer outside than at home, then the government has demonstrated that the rule of law is not adequate protection against political power.

Restrictions imposed by government, or by local monopolists, can make it harder for individuals to find ways to increase productivity and reap the benefits from doing so. (But people are clever about finding ways to get around restrictions; in some countries, there is so much government red tape that a large share of the economy is underground—that is, unregistered, unreported, and unregulated.)

There is plenty of evidence, too, that even government policies intended to be "beneficial"—which often enjoy strong intellectual backing—can impede productivity. Costly mistakes of this kind have included communism and the kind of central planning that held India back until its recent "revolution" and slows its growth to this day. In 1900 Argentina was one of the wealthiest countries in the world; it is generally thought that its relative decline for more than a century now is attributable to government decisions that hampered economic growth. Much of the loss of growth in the United States during the Great Depression resulted from decisions by the government to reduce money supply after the market collapsed in 1929. It is widely believed that Japanese economic stagnation beginning in the 1990s was exacerbated or extended by government policies. So we cannot assume that the leading academic experts and professional economists will understand whatever mistake is stopping growth.

Despite the momentum of the history of the last century, we should recognize that government actions could unintentionally bring economic growth in advanced countries to a stop, or even to a reversal. The economic crisis that began in 2008 hints at the vulnerability of our economic system. Immense costs were imposed on society by a combination of blind and irresponsible business behavior and equally deficient government pursuit of political and ideological goals. We can hope that eventually economic stability and growth will be restored after a few years, just as the costly infla-tion of the 1970s was corrected in about ten years. But there is some real possibility that further mistakes in response to the crisis will make things worse or even indefinitely prevent the economy from being restored. As a society, we don't understand how the economy works—what helps, and what hurts—so it is possible that through misunderstanding we will act in ways that make further growth im-possible, or even put us on a path of long-term decline.

Another class of governmental mistakes can provide relatively easy opportunities to increase productivity and wealth. Consider, for example, the widespread absence of clear titles to land due to weak systems of property registration in some countries. A farmer who owns land but doesn't have a provable title cannot borrow commercially against the security of his land, or sell it for its full value to take advantage of other opportunities. As soon as the government puts in a system that provides a clear title, the value of the land multiplies. Immense amounts of capital can be created, as if out of thin air, by effective and inexpensive titling systems. They require only political will.

Or take the example of a government protecting local farmers by keeping agricultural prices high by restricting imports. France, to take the most obvious example, has sought to protect its farmers and maintain the quality and character of its rural areas, a policy that benefits those who own country houses or who vacation in the countryside. The cost of this policy is paid by French people for whom the high cost of agricultural food is a burden—that is, everybody, but especially the poor.

Indonesia, on the other hand, because its food consumption is growing so fast, could import a great deal of food without damaging its farmers or rural life. Instead, the restriction on imports has had the effect of expanding food production to hillsides and forests, which are environmentally delicate and make inferior cropland. The costs of the policy, in addition to higher food prices, include environmental degradation.

In general, however, the push toward higher productivity acts as a universal, persistent, and reliable force against economic stagnation. The one thing we can count on, in other words, is increasing productivity as an inexorable trend over generations until all countries become modern societies. This isn't to say that productive expansion will proceed uninterrupted. Episodic economic depressions, as Joseph Schumpeter saw, will continue to be inevitable features of growth. None of this, however, will weaken the forces that are bringing a gradual increase in the productivity of human work. The natural pressure toward ever higher productivity will spread from region to region, and eventually the stalled countries will break free and begin to catch up. The countries that continue to grow will exert an ultimately irresistible influence on those that seem left behind. In each country, growth is vulnerable; in the world as a whole, it is an irresistible force.

But the world's least developed region, sub-Saharan Africa, seems to be an exception. While several sub-Saharan African countries have begun to move along the common path to economic growth, most have not. Nicholas Eberstadt has pointed out that recent experience in a number of countries suggests that modernity may not soon spread to the whole world.[2] Some 8 percent of people worldwide live in about two dozen countries that moved backward for the quarter century before 2005—including Haiti and North Korea. The region of sub-Saharan Africa is particularly troubling. Although some of the fifty countries in the region are doing quite well, the region as a whole moved backward by about 10 percent during the last third of a century. Around 10 percent of the world's population live in the region now, but the region is likely to produce much of the world's population growth this century. It is possible that the region will have more than a quarter of the world's population by the end of the twenty-first century.

This record creates two problems for my general thesis. First, does it demonstrate that economic growth is not as easy as I say? Second, how can the whole world become modern in the next two centuries with so many countries moving backward now?

The first question is easier. The countries that are not growing do not have minimum adequate governments. When they achieve such governments, they too will move rapidly along the path to modernity. The lesson from Haiti, North Korea, and sub-Saharan Africa is not that some special qualities are needed for a country to do the learning that is economic and social development. The lesson is that minimum adequate government doesn't come easily and is an absolutely essential prerequisite.

To consider the second question we have to ask how soon, if ever, we should expect these countries to achieve governments good enough to allow economic and social development to begin? Could many or most of these countries remain for centuries as they are now?

Continued poverty in some 10 percent of the world would be problem, but it would not change the nature of the world. If, however, the countries that haven't learned to govern themselves increase their population while the successful part of the world continues to shrink in population, then poverty would be a critical feature of the world, even if it were geographically limited.

Women are having fewer children in sub-Saharan Africa as in the rest of the world, but women there began reducing fertility more recently than in other parts of the world. If recent trends of declin-ing fertility continue, the population of most or all of the region will begin to fall by the end of this century. But in this century the region will probably add between two hundred million and one bil-lion people, while the population of the rest of the world is likely to fall. Sub–Saharan Africa is likely to end the century with between 20 percent and 25 percent of the world's population. If its fertility decline slows down, however, in the twenty-second century sub–Saharan Africa could have more than a third of the world's population.

HOW LONG WILL THE LAGGARDS LAG?

There's no way to predict whether the countries that have not been able to develop adequate government in their first fifty years of in-dependence will succeed in doing so in the next fifty or a hundred years, or whether it will take longer. If they were alone in the world, one would not bet that they would change much for the better in only a century or two. Nor do we know what the balance is between the benefits and harms they get from the rest of the world (say, new technologies versus brain drain).

It is clear that once they do learn to govern themselves, their eco-nomic growth will be much faster and easier because of the outside world. But that opportunity is not yet available to them. Although the outside world has provided immense amounts of financial aid (several times as much per person as the Marshall Plan gave to Eu-rope, but spread over a much longer period), in most cases that aid has served to help inadequate governments remain in power.

The outside world is responsible for improving health conditions in impoverished regions, but this does not necessarily advance the cause of good government. While it is probably not true that the resulting increased population makes it harder for these countries to solve their problems, there is little reason to expect that it makes it easier. More than three decades ago, Professor Julian Simon showed that moderate population growth produces more benefits than costs to a country in the long run,[3] and this has become the mainstream view of economists.

The outside world offers the opportunity for perhaps as many as a few million individuals from stagnating countries to escape each year to join the modern world as immigrants whose children will be natives. Those who escape, however, are likely to be the very people who would have been most useful to their country if they stayed home, so the benefit to the individuals is a cost to their country.

If the rest of the world takes in as much as one quarter of one percent a year of its population as immigrants—a high rate, although less than the U.S. rate in recent years—that would be some fifteen million immigrants a year. If as many as one quarter of those immigrants were from the stagnating countries that would be some four million emigrants a year from those countries. But that huge increase in emigration would be only some 0.3 percent of their population. This is probably the maximum one can imagine without a major change in behavior. This rate of emigration would slow the growth of population in those countries, perhaps enough to prevent them from becoming a very large share of the world population. (If a country's rate of growth for a century is reduced from 0.6 percent a year to 0.3 percent a year, at the end of the century that country will be only 35 percent larger.)

If the conditions of the last fifty years in sub–Saharan Africa continue, there will be an increasing desire in the rest of the world to find ways to help that region to achieve governments that allow them to get on the path of modernization. Unfortunately, nothing is harder for outsiders to do than help a country learn to govern itself. International "helpers" have had a bad record for understanding the real problems of those they are trying to help. It is much easier to "help" by doing things that make the "helper" feel good rather than facing up to the real problems, which usually require patience and politically difficult measures to overcome sick politics in the country in question.

On the other hand, the rest of the world, without any special effort, will provide examples that can influence countries that have not yet found their way. More and more of the world will be adequately governed and democratic. Ordinary people in the lagging countries will come to understand that the rest of the world is different than they are and that they do not have to continue in their old ways. Not only will they see different kinds of countries on television and in the movies, but the millions of their countrymen who have gone abroad to work or live will teach them about how the rest of the world operates. The power of this automatic and unintentional testimony may well be the most important help provided by the outside world. The question is whether the influence of the example of the outside world will be strong enough to make up for the lack of local history of nonviolent politics and of national allegiance.

Our conclusion must be that while we can expect modernity to spread to what is now 90 percent of the world by the end of the next century, it may take another century or two before it comes to the last 10 percent, which by that time may have grown to a quarter or even a half of the world population. This means that while there will be a great reduction in international income inequality among the countries that are now nine-tenths of the world, there will be increasing inequality between all those countries and the 10 percent of the world that will be long delayed by political weakness in starting on their path to modernity, and which will be a much larger part of world population in the future.

MODERNIZATION AND GLOBALIZATION

Modernization is becoming easier to attain as the world becomes more developed and there are more examples of successful behavior to imitate—more countries demonstrating how to act in modern ways, more opportunities for a poor country to use its labor and exports to replace expensive work and products, and more investors seeking out new markets and new sources of labor and supply. Thus globalization makes it harder for islands of inefficiency to survive. As globalization advances, the menu of opportunities for people everywhere expands.

The basic meaning of "globalization," ideology aside, is the growing ability of people everywhere to buy what they need at the best price that exists anywhere in the world and to sell their work wherever in the world people can use it. This sounds like just a matter of better shopping, but it is much more dynamic. Globalization is much more important for producers than for consumers. It means that people trying to produce something can look all over the world for ways to reduce their costs, or to make possible what wasn't possible before. They don't just look at established suppliers with lower prices. They use their imagination and talent to find ways of adapting physical and human resources so they can do better than simply relying on the existing suppliers. This search for more efficiency is a two-way street. Producers search the world to "invent" better suppliers, and at the same time entrepreneurs search the world to find producers for whom they could create a better source of supply for any part of the producer's work.

Among other things, this expansion of markets means that there are constant efforts to find more efficient ways to divide production. Formerly, for example, auto companies manufactured all the components of a car and then assembled and sold the cars. As the inefficiency of this became clear, car companies became assemblers, gradually buying more and more pieces of the car from specialist suppliers making batteries, transmissions, brakes, and other components. These specialist suppliers, originally closely controlled by the car companies, gradually became more independent and competitive. Now almost all parts of the automobile business are potential candidates for outsourcing, including engineering, testing, marketing, and so on. Breaking down all production (including services) so that there is competition concerning each component and sub-component is important because new technology often helps only a small piece of an integrated product, such as a computer. If the computer company makes its own drives, there is no way someone who invents a better drive can put competitive pressure on the company to buy the better drive. But if the computer manufacturer is buying its drives, somebody who makes a better drive has a chance of selling it. So it is easier for new technology—and more creative production processes—to influence final products.

Most of this creative competition between alternative sources goes on within a big country like the United States, but with globalization this source of energy reflects all the different environments found anywhere in the whole world. Globalization vastly increases sources of innovation as it removes barriers to buying and selling from far away. Globalization allows a poor farmer in northeast Thailand to build an irrigation system with capital and technology from the United States and India, produce high-value crops with seeds purchased from international corporations, and sell the crops to modern distributors. Globalization allows these distributors to sell some of the vegetables in Bangkok and other big cities, and then process the rest of the crop for the international market, thus holding down the cost of poor people's food in northern Europe. Globalization allows an American inventor to develop a device to reduce electricity costs—a device made affordable because Chinese factories have learned how to produce complex plastic parts and molds at a fraction of their former cost.

There are, of course, two sides to globalization. One side is the steady movement to reduce the cost of everything, because all elements are bought where they are best or cheapest, and entrepreneurs everywhere are looking for better ways to divide the work. The other side is the spread of competitive pressure on everybody trying to earn a living. Whenever someone can buy for less, it means that someone else has lost a job, because labor is usually the biggest cost. Even if you make the best widget in the world at the lowest price, you may be vulnerable to competition from someone who invents a way to make part of the widget better than you do, or to make the widget unnecessary. The same steady pressure that makes all products, except human time, less expensive and more available also makes earning a living more stressful and all jobs less safe. Not only does globalization and economic development take jobs away—while bringing opportunity and other jobs—but the pressure of competition also erodes traditions, relationships, and ways of life that had developed over generations and may not be replaceable. Overall, the benefits are greater than the costs, but the benefits are spread and the costs are concentrated. In any event, those costs are the costs of modernization, even if it could be done without globalization.

Competition is the ultimate source of efficiency, and as the world gets richer the lash of competition reaches more and more people. The poor farmer of yesterday didn't have much, but he had what he had, which was what his parents had had before him. The modern worker, whether owner, boss, or employee, has much more, but everything he or she has is unsure and may be lost. As countries make the transition from traditional poverty to modern wealth, many people have the worst of both. They don't yet have much, but what they have is precarious, vulnerable to change and competition.

The effect of globalization is to increase the efficiency of world production by producing everything with the best combination of resources from anywhere in the whole world. But globalization will never complete its work. It will always be possible to reduce the costs of distant resources and to find more efficient combinations.

WILL WE RUN OUT OF NATURAL RESOURCES?

With unprecedented increases worldwide in production and wealth, is there any danger that we might run out of natural resources? If the whole world is wealthy, will there be enough oil or clean water? Will we inhabit a polluted landscape that is able to sustain less and less life, not more and more life?

Forty years ago, when the world population was exploding, with growth over two percent a year and no end in sight, there may have been some grounds for fearing that the planet could not provide the raw materials necessary for everyone to be rich. But now that we are approaching a peak population of well under ten billion toward the middle of this century, to be followed by an indefinite period of declining world population, these fears are increasingly recognized as groundless.

In the twentieth century, the world's total annual production grew by twenty times. During this long period of multiplied consumption of natural resources, however, these resources became *less* scarce. That is, the price of almost all raw materials was lower at the end of the century than at the beginning. This includes renewable products like wheat, which cost $10 a bushel in 1900 and only $6 a bushel in 2000 (in constant dollars). It includes traditional metals, like iron and copper, which people have been mining for millennia. Although consumption of these metals rose fivefold during the century, the prices fell by half. It also includes "new" materials like titanium and uranium, which had never been used before, and whose costs fell dramatically as the amount used rose from nothing to millions of pounds per year.

It is true that since we have taken millions of tons of iron out of the earth, there must be less iron than there was before. That is, in some way iron must be scarcer than it was before we mined so much of it. But that is not a realistic way to think about scarcity. There is very little striped toilet paper in the world, but we are not inhibited by the scarcity of striped toilet paper. If people want striped toilet paper, it will be produced. It is not truly scarce; there is as much of it as people want. Despite the multiplied demands of the last century, there was as much of every single raw material as people wanted to buy. The only consistent and realistic measure of scarcity is price. A thing's price shows how much has to be given up or used to get more of that thing. If the price is coming down, then as a practical matter, the material is becoming less scarce. While we have to dig deeper to get our iron today, or separate it from much more useless rock than we used to, the cost of the work of getting iron from the ground is less than it used to be. Iron, like almost all raw materials, is becoming *less* scarce.

It is likely that the twentieth century will turn out to be the century with the greatest growth of world production. Population at the end of the twentieth century was six times larger than it was at the beginning of the century. In the twenty-first century, population will only grow by perhaps 50 percent before it starts falling. If the huge growth in use of raw materials in the twentieth century did not increase scarcity, there is no reason that slower increases in consumption in the future should make raw materials expensive enough to stand in the way of economic growth.

Of course, the fact that raw materials have been becoming less scarce since the beginning of history doesn't mean they will necessarily continue to get less scarce in the future. (But those people who confidently predict such scarcity should be asked why they think the future will be unlike the past in this way.) It is also true that some raw materials, such as whale oil, have become so scarce that we don't use them anymore. But we don't need them any more either. The key fact is that we don't spend much of our income on raw materials. Only some 15 percent of world income goes to buy all the raw materials that are used, so even if the long-term experience of falling raw material costs were reversed, and costs began to go up, it would be a long time before people would be seriously hurt by increasing raw material scarcity.

But what about the pollution problem? Will not the great increase in waste products produced by a rich world of seven or eight billion people harm the environment? The brief answer is that people today and in the future have the power to decide how much to protect the environment; no inevitable result of future wealth requires that the environment become worse than it is now.

We can get some perspective from a little history. Because of their polluted environment a few centuries ago, cities like London were deathtraps where the population could only be maintained by a steady influx of people from the countryside. Human filth, horse excrement, and coal smoke made cities unimaginably dirty and dangerous to health.

The historical pattern is clear, repeated again and again all over the world. First there is poverty and clean air. Then there is industrialization and dirty air (and water). Then there is wealth and clean air. When societies get rich, they choose to spend the resources necessary to protect their environment. By almost all measures, the U.S. environment, for example, has been growing less polluted for well over a generation.

Basically, the world is like a family home or a country. It will be kept as clean as the people involved can agree to keep it. Decisions about how much to spend to keep things clean are more complicated in the world. But there are no physical or economic reasons why people of the future cannot afford to have an environment as least as clean as it is today, even with many more people and much more wealth.[4]

However, no one can know whether people someday will be afflicted with some form of pollution that causes damage before it is well enough understood to act against it. There is no reason that this has to happen, but presumably it could. In fact, today it is common to hear that CO_2 and other potential causes of global warming are examples of such pollutants.

THE QUESTION OF GLOBAL WARMING

Many people believe that the planet is warming at an alarming rate. Increased carbon levels in the atmosphere create a "greenhouse effect," with higher temperatures, melting ice caps, and rising seas. Could this warming produce such devastation globally that modernization is derailed?

There is no doubt that there was global warming in the twentieth century, mostly in the first part of the century, though there was no statistically significant warming between 1995 and 2010. It is possible that human activity is responsible for at least some of the warming.

The three principal questions are: Is nature (the sun, say, or geologic cycles of warming and cooling) or human activity the primary cause of the observed warming? Will the likely warming be good or bad for human life? If human activity is the primary cause of the warming, and further warming will be harmful, is a major effort now to reduce carbon emissions a sensible way to solve the problem?

There is no clear scientific answer to the question of whether nature or mankind is the primary cause of the observed warming. There is good evidence and theory showing that in the past nature has frequently produced this much warming and more. There is little if any comparable physical or historical evidence that human activity could cause the observed warming, although there are computer models and much theoretical work supporting the possibility of human causation. The computer models have not been able yet to make successful predictions, however, and all scientists recognize that they do not sufficiently reflect some of the important influences, such as water vapor.

The pattern of warming to be expected from natural causes may well be different from the pattern to be expected from the current theories about anthropogenic global warming (AGW). But while some scientific work on this has been done, it is not clear yet whether the warming that has occurred is closer to the fingerprint of past natural warming or to the fingerprint of the AGW theory.

Much of the discussion of global warming seems to ignore the fact that the world's temperature has never been constant. The world is always either warming or cooling (or both on different time scales). This raises the question of what temperature we should prefer? It is clear that much colder would be very bad—think ice age. It is also clear that much warmer would be bad. On the basis of both history and analysis, it is likely that a little warming would on balance be beneficial and a little cooling would on balance be harmful, though of course either change would have both good and bad effects. It is also possible that, whatever the cause of the recent warming, the world will face a serious danger from naturally caused cooling in the coming centuries, but currently there is no way to estimate the timing or degree of this risk.

How should we respond to the problem if we conclude that AGW will cause a harmful amount of warming (either by itself or added to natural warming)? A number of experts, including some who believe that AGW is dangerous, have made a strong case that the expensive proposals to reduce carbon emissions do not make sense now because the benefits these proposals are expected to bring are not nearly large enough to justify the cost. Bjorn Lomberg, for example, speaking for an eminent group that has analyzed the alternatives, argues that many more lives could be saved (through increased cancer research, for example) and other benefits attained with a fraction of the money proposed to reduce carbon emissions, even if the calculations of the believers in AGW are correct. He and others also argue that more reduction of AGW could be achieved by spending now on research and development to create better ways to prevent or counter carbon releases than by relying on currently known methods of reducing atmospheric CO_2.

Despite a number of uncertainties, we can have reasonable confidence that the world will overcome the problem of global warming at a cost that is not large enough to significantly influence the drive toward modernization. The main question is, how many resources will be wasted by unwise responses to the potential danger? But these are short-term issues. A longer-term concern is what the extraordinary amount of political influence on scientific and technical questions regarding AGW says about decision-making in the future. Although the environment can be kept as clean and safe as we collectively choose, experience with the AGW question suggests that modern societies may not necessarily do a good job of making decisions about how to accomplish their goals.

WHAT CAN WE LEARN FROM MODERNIZATION?

There are two centuries of experience with modernization. We can see that Asian as well as European countries have already completed the passage to modernity. We see that some countries from all regions and cultures have moved a good way along the path to modernization. This includes Muslim countries like Indonesia, Turkey, and Malaysia; sub−Saharan countries like Ghana; and Latin American countries like Chile and Colombia. So we learn that many more countries are likely to become modern, too.

But we also see that many countries have not really started on the path to becoming modern, though they have some of the benefits of modernity. We also see countries like Argentina and Cuba, which once were well along the path to development, stagnating and falling far behind. So we learn that modernization is not just for some narrow group of special countries, nor is it automatic and guaranteed for everyone.

We also see that overall, the pace of growth is uneven. Per capita growth for the whole world was nearly three percent a year from

1950 to 1973, but just a little more than half as fast from 1973 to 2003 (although faster in the last years of the period). Only Asia, led by China and India, grew faster after 1973 than in the twenty-three years before 1973. Lucas's model of later starters catching up reflects reality only for the world as a whole, not for each country.

It seems clear that unless there is a drastic and unprecedented change for the worse, much of the world will continue moving along the path to modernity. The real questions are: How fast? How many will be left behind?

China and India together are nearly half of the not-yet-modern population of the world. They seem to be clearly on the way to achieving modernity, probably near the end of this century. There doesn't seem to be any reason not to expect that at least half the rest of the population of the world will follow closely behind China and India (and some even ahead), so a cautious and skeptical projection would judge that some three-quarters of the world will be at least up to current Southern European levels of development by early in the next century, though many countries might not by then have achieved fully post-industrial economies.

At the beginning of the twenty-first century, only about 15 percent of the world was modern. By the end of the century, 75 percent of the world will be modern or almost modern. That immense change is almost certain to happen. It doesn't require any acceleration of growth; in fact, it can happen even if the pace of growth is slower than it has been.

Clearly, most of the next century will be overwhelmingly dominated by modern countries. The big story will no longer be the passage to modernity, because most of the world will have completed its passage. In the twenty-second century the concern about modernization will be what, if anything, should be done about the part of the world that hasn't made it yet.

We can't know now exactly how the problem of the not-yet-modern will look to the world in the next century. Undoubtedly, everybody will assume that the normal and right outcome will be that the whole world should be modern. It may be clear by then that the countries that haven't made it yet are on their way, requiring a few decades or generations to complete the passage. But it is quite possible that there will be a group of problematic countries that seem incapable of taking the path to modernity.

Countries that don't become modern by the early part of the next century may pose a threat to rest of the world. A big country like Pakistan or Nigeria, whose population and institutions has not yet been shaped by the experience of modern life, could pose a challenge to the modern part of the world. Probably, though, the main concern of the modern world will be to accelerate movement to modernity of the minority that has been left behind, to speed the day when the whole world is modern.

When you think about it, the question of when the "whole world" will be modern is not so important. Once three-quarters of the world is modern, and much of the rest is on the way, it will be the modern part of the world that counts.

Until recently, people assumed that life would remain the way it had always been. Today, people all over the world believe that change is possible, that their actions can change their destinies. This simple belief looses a great flood of human energy and imagination. It is the fundamental source of the power that cannot be stopped from gradually transforming the world. This power can be resisted in some places, perhaps even for decades or more, but it will always break out someplace else, and eventually it will overcome resistance everywhere.

Increasing productivity—a process that has become both natural and inevitable—is the underlying engine of that modernizing force. The combination of people who want to make their lives better, and the plenitude of opportunities to improve productivity that exist everywhere, produce a constant tide of pressure for development, and will continue to do so at least until all countries have become modern, and probably long after. Modernity may or may not be desirable, but it is inexorable. The masses have voted, so to speak, and unless they change their mind, or unless those who haven't yet voted are very different from those who have already voted, the human desire to be modern is too strong to resist. We have the ability to shape and to influence the character of the modern world, but not to prevent it.

NOTES

1. Angus Maddison, *Contours of the World Economy 1-2030 AD: Essays in Macro-Economic History* (Oxford University Press, 2007).

2. Nicholas Eberstadt, "The Global Poverty Paradox," *Commentary* (October, 2010).

3. Julian Simon, *The Economics of Population Growth* (Princeton: Princeton University Press, 1977).

4. These issues are discussed more fully in my book, *Passage to a Human World* (New Brunswick, NJ: Transaction, 1989).

3

FREEDOM

Why a Modern Society Can't Be a Tyranny (for Long)

L ooking back over the last two hundred years of human history, one is struck by three massive changes: the multiplication of population, the spread of vast amounts of wealth created by new kinds of work, and the increase in human freedom.

Before 1800, the world was an authoritarian place. The first small wave of democratization, which had its origins in England and the United States, crested and fell back in the nineteenth century, and by the start of the twentieth century only a handful of democracies existed.

A second wave arose after World War II and brought democratic change to such countries as West Germany, Italy, Japan, South Korea, Greece, India, and Israel. Still, in 1974 only thirty-nine countries (or a quarter of the world's independent nations) were democratic. A third wave of democratization began in the late 1970s in Latin America, and in the late 1980s in what had been the Communist world, with the result that today some two-thirds of the world's countries elect their top leaders.

Between 1985 and today, scores of countries have made transitions toward democracy. According to "Freedom in the World, 2010," the annual Freedom House report, 89 of 193 countries, with 46 percent of the world's population, were "free," meaning that their citizens possessed substantial protection of civil and political rights.

Political modernization is part of the learning process countries go through as part of learning to be modern. Modern democracies demonstrate to countries still in the throes of political development what their own future can be and how to get there. As totalitarian states have withered away, and as liberal democracy has emerged victorious over fascism and communism, the percentage of people living under democratic government has dramatically expanded. Although there have been setbacks to democracy—in Russia, sub-Saharan Africa, the non-Baltic former Soviet Union, Venezuela, and other South American countries—it is becoming clear that democracy is not something that belongs to Europe, or to the United States, or to the West. Eastern and Muslim and Slavic societies also incorporate the fundamentals of democracy. Authoritarianism has largely fallen into disrepute. The challenges to democracy from fascism and communism have been defeated.

There remain two principal forces of resistance to worldwide democracy. The most important is antimodernist ideology, which is today represented by those Islamic leaders who assert that Muslims must reject democracy because democracy puts secular law and public opinion before Shariah and submission to Allah's scripture. The Islamic challenge to democracy is discussed in chapter 5. Here it is enough to note that a number of Muslim-majority countries—such as Indonesia, Turkey, and Pakistan—have democratic institutions and varying degrees of real democracy; they do not accept the principle that Islam is incompatible with democracy. Even the radical Islamist regime in Iran has provided a place in its system for popular elections, and the Iranian public's feelings about the illegitimacy of interference in elections has galvanized the strongest opposition to the regime so far.

The second obstacle is authoritarian regimes, which may claim to be democratic but in fact deny their citizens real elections and civil rights. Communism has been the most systematic example of this kind of resistance to real democracy, but in Venezuela and elsewhere populist fascists also pay lip service to democracy while operating tyrannies.

Although democracy does not always work the first time it is tried in a country, and although there are many grossly defective democracies that don't become reasonably full democracies for generations, the overall tendency globally is for countries to move toward democracy. With the partial exception of Islam, there is no competing conception of how government should be run or what makes a government legitimate. People all over the world believe that the source of political legitimacy is the people and law, and that people should be free to express their own ideas and compete for political power without fear.

BASIC ASPECTS OF DEMOCRACY IN THE LONG-TERM FUTURE

What can we expect when the whole world has become modern?

First we should recognize the defects of democracy in the best, most advanced, and most democratic countries. Theoretically, democracy gives power to citizens, but in practice that is not how a modern country works. It is not practical for the people to decide all the questions the government must answer. Most people don't care about most of the questions. They often don't even know what they want and rarely have the information needed to make an intelligent decision.

In principle, people act through their elected representatives. Most representatives, however, are often as ignorant and uninterested and powerless as the voters. Furthermore, most people who are elected do not act primarily as representatives of those who elected them. When confronted with problems of governance, representatives do not sit down and ask, "What do my voters want me to do?" There are just too many things for a representative to worry about to have time to think about what the voters want. So the theoretical justification for democracy doesn't square very well with the facts about how democracies actually work.

There is, however, an important connection between the theory of popular sovereignty and the reality of modern government. Occasionally voters become very dissatisfied with how the government is acting and rise up to shake the political balance and force change.

Although this happens very rarely, perhaps every few decades in any large polity, the potential for such a public uprising influences political behavior and is an important protector of democratic values. Obviously, something that operates so rarely can only protect against the worst failings; it cannot keep the system clean.

Almost all governmental decisions involve a mixture of two questions: how to be wise in the game we all play against nature, and how to choose among the interests of various parts of the population. The game against nature involves choosing, for example, ways of producing electricity that minimize economic and environmental costs. But many people who seek to influence society's choices are concerned not with the best or most efficient solution but with the one that serves their interests—as members of a union, investors, adherents to some ideology, or whatever. Almost everything a government can do is better for some people than it is for others. Any decision will make some people happy and others unhappy.

The basic test of a stable system of government is that it doesn't cause enough unhappiness to create a revolution and meets minimum standards of civility and respect toward those who do not have the power to protect themselves. In other words, the main long-term requirement of a political system is that it must prevent any group with the power to destroy internal peace and stability from being too unhappy about the government, by making sure that any such group is able to get enough of what it wants so that it is no worse than "sullen but not mutinous."

This is what Judge Learned Hand argued some eighty years ago in his essay "Democracy: Its Presumptions and Reality." While our democracy, said Hand, does not in reality empower the "will of the people," if such a concept has any practical meaning, it does provide "a bloodless measure of social forces—bloodless, have you thought of that?—a means of continuity, a principle of stability, a relief from the paralyzing terror of revolution." In democracies, as in other forms of government, people continually come into conflict, but the losers have no fear of death or banishment. In practically all cases, violence plays no role in influencing government decisions. We may not like the way politics works, and we may be disappointed with the decisions it produces, but for the vast majority of people there is no better alternative. According to Hand,

> Given an opportunity to impose our will, a ground where we may test our mettle, we get the sense that there is some propriety in yielding to those who impose upon us. There has been an outlet, a place of reckoning, a means not of counting heads, but of matching wit and courage. If these are fairly measured, most of us acquiesce; we are conscious of a stronger power which it is idle to resist, until we in turn have organized in more formidable array and can impress ourselves in turn.[1]

Government behavior must be determined primarily by politics—not by reason, or morality—and politics can be better or worse than we see it today, but it can never approach the ideal. It will rarely produce decisions that come close to the best way to play the game against nature. All government decisions of any importance will involve complex and heated political struggles. Often the price is that decisions produced by politics result in less justice, less efficiency, or less safety than we would want. The result can even be war or depression. In the case of environmentalist excesses, such as refusal to allow use of DDT against malaria-carrying mosquitoes in Africa, the result can be millions of deaths. If some views about global warming are correct, wrong decisions about climate could cause disastrous rises in sea level, or a new ice age. Nonetheless, there is no democratic alternative to politics for making decisions. Political struggle is as much a consequence of political freedom as economic competition is a consequence of economic freedom. The political system simply must produce outcomes that do not destroy support for the political system, whatever the cost in "efficiency."

The essential task of politics is to divide rewards and burdens among all the elements of society in ways that allow the society and the political system to continue. There are many ways in which this can be done. The nature of future democratic governments in modern societies is a very open question and likely to be the subject of a good deal of (non-military) conflict.

First, there will continue to be experimentation and conflict about how much decision-making should be assigned to government—that is to say, to politics—and how much should be left to markets, non-governmental social mechanisms, and individuals. We have for many years been going through a phase in which most people, especially most highly educated people, naturally assume that laws and government are able to change society to reduce evils and improve performance. It may be that this belief will continue and government will be given more and more responsibility, regardless of how well it discharges the responsibilities it already has. It is also possible that the inherent weaknesses of political decision-making and bureaucratic implementation will become more strongly appreciated, even while experience enables society to reduce them. So some countries may move in the direction of reducing the role of government and politics in dealing with social problems (or at least move responsibility to more local levels).

Another kind of variation is that different democracies will emphasize different sources of power. That is, in some countries the main source of power will be the ability to influence a consensus among non-elected groups that have gained a dominant position. Such contenders for influence include university faculties, media leaders, judges, non-governmental organizations (NGOs), and bureaucrats. This is a very broad and diverse set of elements. From time to time, and from issue to issue and country to country, different elements of the class of intellectual leaders will have the most strength and the most institutional power compared to those whose power is the result of elections.

A third variation is that different democracies will give greater or lesser power to elected representatives. Now, in all democracies power is theoretically based on legislators, executives, and judges who are either elected to office or appointed (in most cases) by elected officials. The question is how much of that power based on elections is overcome by institutions and practices that give practical power to others. For example, how much is the bureaucracy able to protect itself from political control? How much do judges in their interpretation of statutes or constitutions put their own preferences over the decisions of legislators or voters? How much are moneyed interests able to use wealth to gain political power? How much are unions or industrial groups able to limit the ability of elected government to make decisions in their areas of interest?

Power or authority can also be transferred away from elected officials to outside organizations, such as the United Nations or international functional organizations such as the World Health Organization, or societies of jurists. In such cases, elected officials are committed to obeying some authority not elected by their citizens. They may maintain some theoretical power to withdraw the authority given to the outside institution, but the reality may be that real decision-making power is stripped from the elected officials.

Although elections and majority rule are today almost universally accepted as the basis of democratic legitimacy, the kind of democracy that is inherent in modern life is not necessarily the democracy in which power derives from elections. Rather, a state is democratic when it permits open competition for political power; gives all citizens the possibility of gaining influence or power not by force but by harnessing their energies, skills, and determination; protects the basic political rights afforded the individual; grants meaningful inclusion of individuals and diverse groups; and allows organized opposition and public disagreement.

This is not to imply that modernization generally or democratization in particular can be interpreted as Westernization. There will be a great variety of political possibilities in the modern world, and there may well be considerable struggle and change among competing systems. The future will likely see evolution and experimentation with various forms of democracy, and a wide range of trajectories toward democratization as nations figure out how to design degrees of federalism and internationalism, how to reconcile sometimes competing democratic values, and how to balance political, bureaucratic, legal, and professional sources of authority. Democratic values can be weighted in different ways, and cannot all be maximized at the same time. Equality—of result or opportunity—can be pursued more or less intensely, as can freedom from governmental interference, and protection of different kinds of property and a variety of other kinds of rights. Democracies can strike different balances between symbolic and practical concerns, and exhibit different degrees of concern about the protection of national interests and security. Within the democratic future there is much history yet to be written.

WHY TO BE MODERN IS TO BE DEMOCRATIC

The most obvious feature of a democracy is that it is not a tyranny. The power of democratic governments does not rest on censorship, jailing dissidents, suppressing opposition by force, or limiting the freedoms of speech, assembly, and political organization. In a tyranny, a closed group from which the majority is excluded maintains control through generations by employing violence or the threat of violence. In this sense, "democracy" may be used as a shorthand for "non-tyranny."

But what has democracy to do with modernization?

The answer can be put quite simply: democracy will come to be virtually universal in the modern world, because the very same process that generates modern wealth also encourages democracy. With only very rare exceptions, the modernization process fosters the kind of political cultures that are essential preconditions of effective democracy (or at least non-tyranny). Democracy has such broad appeal and inherent fitness to modern conditions that it will become the preferred form of government for almost everyone.[2]

To see why an effective modern society is by its very nature incompatible with tyranny, it is useful to begin with some characteristics of societies that produce—and are fashioned by—modern economies.

First, from Brazil to the Philippines to South Korea to Taiwan, economic development creates a substantial, politically empowered, well-educated, urban middle class—professionals, businesspeople, civil servants, managers, shopkeepers, teachers—that seeks accountable democratic government. (As in Barrington Moore's dictum, "No bourgeoisie, no democracy.")

The requirements of operating a modern country mean that this class will be at least moderately educated and informed about the world. As GDP per capita grows, the middle class widens—and this is a class for which success more often than not rests on the ability to build trust and to elicit cooperation from diverse groups of people. Samuel Huntington posited that economic development increases the numbers of literate and educated citizens who "develop characteristics of trust, satisfaction, and competence that go with democracy." Modern knowledge societies—in which the main sources of economic change are innovative ideas—cannot function effectively without highly educated publics that have become accustomed to thinking for themselves, questioning hierarchical authority, and demanding political and civil rights. For a concrete example, take the expectation that property rights will be protected in a democratic regime. Mancur Olson in *Rise and Decline of Nations* writes:

> An economy will be able to reap all potential gains from investment and from long-term transactions only if it has a government that is believed to be both strong enough to last and inhibited from violating individual rights to property and rights to contract enforcement . . . Interestingly, the conditions that are needed to have the individual rights needed for maximum economic development are exactly the same conditions that are needed to have a lasting democracy.[3]

In short, citizens who are accustomed to exercising free choice in their personal lives can be expected to demand the same right in the political sphere and to press for liberal democracy. For a while they may be satisfied with economic advance, but before very long they will begin increasing the pressure for political rights. Economic development, in other words, intensifies demands for the political benefits of democracy.

Second, economic development, as we've suggested earlier, brings in its wake profound cultural and value changes. In modern societies economic success derives from the creativity and initiative of citizens working in environments that encourage innovation and grant expansive freedoms. To be freely innovative, in turn, requires a habit of skepticism and an unwillingness simply to accept the authority of tradition or social pressure.

Take, for example, a small modern society in the Middle East. In their recent book *Startup Nation,* Dan Senor and Saul Singer ask how Israel—a country of seven million, only sixty years old, surrounded by enemies, with no natural resources—could produce more start-up companies and attract more venture capital than nations like Japan, China, India, Korea, Canada, and the United Kingdom, and how Israel could have more companies on the NASDAQ stock exchange than any country outside the United States. They answer that Israel's strength lies partly in its informal and antihierarchical culture of individualism, self-reliance, and a disinclination to accept authority and rank.[4] This kind of culture demands democracy.

Not only do modern citizens enjoy a broad range of choices both as consumers and in building their careers, but their society is built on the open exchange and transfer of information. Modern countries, after all, depend on the flow of information as much as the free flow of goods. Technological innovations enable citizens to enjoy access to easy communication with hundreds or thousands of other people in their own country and abroad, and make it more difficult for their governments to withhold information.

These expectations and habits of mind associated with a modern orientation will work to cumulative political effect. In the future, as more countries become democratic, people will find it ever more difficult to regard as legitimate any kind of government other than democracy. It will be virtually impossible in such societies, populated by people with those habits, people used to a good measure of economic and political freedom, to achieve and sustain the kind of tyranny or authoritarian regime that has been common in the world until recently.

Third, modernization brings about increasingly complex economies—with sources of power and wealth outside the state, and openness to foreign trade—that are extremely difficult for authoritarian regimes to control. In authoritarian regimes, political monopoly is typically linked with economic monopoly. So it is almost impossible for an authoritarian government to permit the kinds of freedom needed for economic success.

Democracies, in turn, outperform authoritarian countries in the long run because they encourage openness and adaptability. The striking phenomenon of modern countries moving away from authoritarian expectations and toward democracy is not just a matter of coincidence or fashion; it reflects the fact that modern economies gain a competitive advantage from democratic values and expectations. If a society did not have many people with these values and expectations, it would not have produced a modern economy. If, too, a society ceases to produce these kinds of people, its economy will lose its competitive advantage and begin to fall further and further behind other societies.

This is not to say that there exists an absolute or deterministic relation between industrialization and political liberty. Economic growth and political freedom are positively correlated, but a nondemocratic state can experience robust economic growth (like Singapore today, Japan before 1945, and the Soviet Union during the 1950s and 1960s). Experience shows that relatively poor countries can grow extraordinarily rapidly when they have a strong dictator who pursues sound economic policies. Such growth, however, lasts only for the ruling span of one or two dictators. Other states, like India, are democratic but not economically modern. (The democratic revolutions in France and the United States, too, took place before either country had modernized economically.) In some places (like South Korea), economic growth will precede political development. Newly democratizing countries such as Indonesia or Bangladesh may be vulnerable to temporary regressions in the direction of authoritarianism. Sometimes economic integration can prompt political fragmentation (for example, the demands for autonomy heard from the Basques, Tamils, Tibetans, Palestinians, Kurds, Chechens, and Kosovars). Along the way, too, democracy and increased economic production may come into conflict, as during periods of anti-economic populism, or when a less-than-democratic regime maintains good fiscal discipline.

What we can say is that *in the long run* there is an ironclad correlation between development and democracy. The two processes reinforce one another: economic development brings changes conducive to democracy, and democracy, in turn, makes more economic growth possible. The point is that modernization brings social and cultural changes that make democratization increasingly probable, and that economic growth creates the necessary preconditions for democracy. "It was only the prospect of economic growth in which everyone prospered," Irving Kristol writes, "if not equally or simultaneously, that gave modern democracies their legitimacy and durability."[5] The relationship between democracy and productivity is so strong that we can go even further: not only does wealth bring democracy but the very social behaviors and changes required to produce wealth—an emphasis on freedom, tolerance of diversity, and participation—would themselves produce democracy, were it not already in place.

Non-democratic countries may possess many features of modern countries. A modern society can stay mildly authoritarian for at least a generation or two, but no modern society can remain a non-democracy for very long. Experience gives good grounds to expect that if a country becomes modern in most ways—principally, economically—then the characteristics it has acquired will eventually move it along the road to democracy. Of the more than twenty modern countries today, only one of them, Singapore, is not yet democratic. Singapore's authoritarianism has not yet lasted beyond the life of its founder, Lee Kuan Yu, a moderate man of great talent whose leadership authority is partly based on his role in transforming his small country from poverty to wealth and freeing it from Malay domination. And his country is only mildly authoritarian.

By way of illustrating the relationship between development and democracy, we might linger for a moment on the example of China, which is not yet a modern country, though it has strong modern sectors. Since Deng Xiaoping's reforms in the late 1970s, China has seen substantial economic liberalization, including the limited restoration of private property, but political authoritarianism has continued. Much of the country's rural population is not yet integrated into the modern economy (some 40 percent of the population is still engaged in agriculture); neither life expectancy nor education have yet reached modern levels. Much of the modern sector, meanwhile, is distorted by government financing and control. The rule of law is weak and high-level corruption plays a central role in accommodating market economy behavior to communist control. Unlike Singapore, which could make a smooth transition to democracy with no great social shock, ending the Communist Party control of China may not happen without a period of great turmoil. China will not become modern until the strong incompatibility between China's political and economic development is resolved.[6]

SOFT TYRANNY

Modern countries are infertile ground for what the French political thinker Alexis de Tocqueville called "hard tyranny." But they may be susceptible to what Tocqueville regarded as the distinctively modern phenomenon of "soft tyranny": a bureaucratic state run by benevolent "schoolmasters," who create an "orderly, gentle, peaceful slavery" under the command of "administrative despotism." As Jean-François Revel put it:

> Tocqueville the visionary predicted with stunning precision the coming ascension of the omnipresent, omnipotent and omniscient state the twentieth-century man knows so well: the state as protector, entrepreneur, educator; the physician-state, impresario-state, bookseller-state, helpful and predatory, tyrant and guardian, banker, father and jailer all at once . . . Its power borders on the absolute partly because it is scarcely felt, having increased by imperceptible stages at the wish of its subjects, who turned to it instead of to each other.[7]

In a Tocquevillian soft tyranny, elected political leaders are smothered in a blanket of restrictions. Such a regime would retain the practical virtues of democracy, although citizens would seek to affect policy by influencing not politicians or legislators but bureaucrats or NGOs. We may see a form of soft tyranny in a future European Union in which national legislatures have as a practical matter lost power.

Political institutions not solidly rooted in the popular vote suffer from two disadvantages. First, ordinary people feel more and more excluded as political institutions weaken, for weak political institutions respond less well to dissatisfaction among citizens. However, if a government bases its power and self-image on commitment to coddling citizens, there may be less danger of explosive dissatisfaction. The institutions of such a regime may develop their own, non-political ways of responding to pockets of building resentment.

The second disadvantage of a political authority that is less responsive to popular vote has to do with legitimacy. Governments are commonly justified by the fact that they exist by the consent of the governed. In a traditional democracy, people explain to themselves that they should obey the government and its laws because they themselves elected the government officials who made the laws—and they can un-elect those officials in due course. It may be more difficult to believe this if government becomes even less representative than it is today.

WORLD GOVERNMENT

So far I have discussed the political features of modernization as if the world will continue to be organized into separate countries. Does this assumption betray a lack of imagination? Will there even be *countries* as we know them in the indefinite future? When the whole world is modern would a world government arise?

In some respects, the question is moot, since many characteristics of the modern world are independent of political organization. Long life, education, comfortable and safe living conditions, work in an international and commercial environment, and protection from the ravages of nature will characterize the future whether there is a single sovereign government in the world or a thousand countries.

The political dimensions of the modern world, however, are another matter. Here, four broad possibilities present themselves:

1. A single world government arises with the unquestioned right to command all local units of government.
2. There remains some variant of the current world, in which authority is distributed among a fairly large number of nation-states of various sizes.
3. The large nation-states could be broken into a much larger number of smaller sovereign countries, leaving no superpowers.
4. Or, conversely, the change could be toward fewer and larger states, with regional governments like a European Union assuming authority over member states.

There is nothing about the nature of modern life that requires world government or inclines in its favor. Indeed, an important effect of modernization is that it eliminates one of the main arguments people have used in favor of world government: that it could prevent war, since it would enjoy a monopoly on the ultimate forms of force. But once the prospect of war no longer looms, for reasons discussed in chapter 4, the strongest motivation for promoting world government will dissipate.

The most reliable protection against abuse by government is competition from other governments. In a modern world of wealthy, free, and competent people, government is one of the few forces likely to be strong enough to cause large-scale, long-lasting harm, even without a tyranny of coercion. If it is recognized that the danger of a world government is too great, and its advantages too doubtful and limited, then the question becomes: what system of states would be politically strong enough to resist the natural tendency of bureaucratic forces toward consolidation of power into a world government?

It does seem likely that in the modern world, or during the current transition, there will be a strong inclination toward world government. Many students today are taught that nationalism breeds belligerence. In the modern world, a drift toward world government may also be propelled by advocates of rationalization and simplification. Reformers will talk about how difficult it is to convince dozens or hundreds of national governments to adopt uniform measures to improve the human condition. They will suggest that nations can keep lower-level governments with all the familiar symbols and rituals, but that these lower-level governments must be subject to the decisions of the world government on any matters that have international effects or where the conscience of humankind is affronted by local custom.

The only countervailing force against the drift toward world government would be supplied by the citizens of nation-states whose traditions and emotional attachments produce strong loyalty. Now the fact that there are great differences between countries that are at very different stages on the common path to modernity makes the idea of world government seem impractical. When essentially the whole world has become modern, the idea of a common government will seem less objectionable and become more tempting, if no less dangerous. It will only be resisted if people have strong attachments to their own country.[8]

In raising questions about soft tyranny and world government, we have traveled pretty far along the road to modernity. These questions are not about whether the world will become democratic; they are questions about the various forms worldwide democracy might take. The histories of the twenty-odd countries that are already modern, and developments in many non-modern countries (India, Brazil), strongly suggest that the day is indeed coming when all people shall have those freedoms we call democracy, and, for most of the world, that day will come within this century.

NOTES

1. Learned Hand, "Democracy: Its Presumptions and Reality," in *The Spirit of Liberty* (New York: Vantage, 1959).

2. I am far from the first to notice that as nations learn to achieve high productivity, they typically also learn to be democratic, nor am I the

first to present economic development as a necessary but not a sufficient condition of democratic development. The sociologist Seymour Martin Lipset, for instance, concluded that "economic development involving industrialization, urbanization, high educational standards, and a steady increase in the overall wealth of the society, is a basic condition sustaining democracy." Thus it is no coincidence that Spain, Portugal, and Greece experienced unprecedented rapid economic growth just before their transitions to democracy.

3. Mancur Olson, *Rise and Decline of Nations* (New Haven: Yale, 1982).

4. Dan Senor and Saul Singer, *Startup Nation* (New York: Twelve, 2009).

5. Irving Kristol, "The Neoconservative Persuasion," *The Weekly Standard* 8:47 (August 25, 2003).

6. This claim is falsifiable. If China's economic growth continues so that the entire Chinese population achieves modern living standards and education but the government continues to be controlled by the authoritarian Communist Party, we will have to admit that our understanding of how the modern world works is misguided. If China's rapid growth rates continue for a generation—which may be less than likely—that test might arrive as soon as the middle of this century. I make the following prediction: When high school education and high life expectancy have spread throughout China, and it has become an urban society operating a competitive commercial economy with less than ten percent of the population working the land, China will no longer be a one-party state that prevents or oppresses political opposition and denies freedom of speech and of religion. If this prediction does not come to pass, my understanding of the nature of modern countries is wrong.

7. Jean-François Revel, *How Democracies Perish* (Garden City, NY: Doubleday, 1984).

8. This argument is made by Natan Sharansky and Shira Wolosky Weiss in *Defending Identity: Its Indispensable Role in Protecting Democracy* (New York: Public Affairs, 2008).

4

THE DECLINE AND FALL OF THE WAR SYSTEM

For all of history, war and violence have been central aspects of human life. At least from the earliest recorded times, more than four thousand years ago, to the devastating World Wars in the twentieth century, war has seemed to be an inevitable result of human aggression.

As long as there have been states, preparations for war, or efforts to avoid war, have been central considerations for national policy (except for a few countries like New Zealand). Almost exactly a century ago, after reviewing the British fleet as First Lord of the Admiralty, Winston Churchill remarked on the centrality of military power to the life of nations:

> For consider these ships . . . They were all that we had. On them . . . floated the might, majesty, dominion and power of the British Empire. All our long history built up century after century . . . all the means of livelihood and safety of our faithful, industrious, active population depended on them. Open the sea-cocks and let them sink beneath the surface, . . . and in a few minutes . . . the whole outlook of the world would be changed. The British Empire would dissolve like a dream.[1]

From time immemorial, the "war system" has been the foundation of international relations. Each nation understood that unless it either had sufficient military force to defend itself or was part of an alliance capable of providing protection, it would be compelled to comply with demands made upon it by other nations or would risk invasion. No government could fulfill its responsibilities unless its military was strong enough and the relationships of the major powers were balanced in a way that provided protection.

For centuries England, for example, followed a policy of using its influence (and military force, when necessary) to ensure that no one power could dominate Europe, by supporting the rivals of whatever country threatened to predominate—Spain, then France, then Germany. A constant diplomatic dance of alliances ensured that no group was strong enough to overpower the others. The key measure of value for countries in the politics of alliance building was military power. Therefore, even countries with no apparent defensive needs and no interest in aggression had an important incentive to build and maintain potent military forces in order to maximize their international influence.

One of the consequences of the balance-of-power system was that conflicts about small matters between countries from rival blocs could easily escalate into major war. The classic modern example is World War I, which was sparked when Serbian nationalists assassinated Austrian Archduke Francis Ferdinand. Austria-Hungary, which was already armed with Germany's pledge of support, declared war on Serbia, which in turn caused Russia to mobilize against Austria-Hungary, after which Germany declared war against France and invaded Belgium. Although Great Britain did not have an interest one way or the other in the fate of Serbia, it had committed to defend Belgium, and so declared war on Germany. Thus the stage was set for an unprecedentedly bloody war between the Central Powers (Germany, Austria-Hungary, and Turkey) and the Allies (France, Great Britain, Russia, Italy, and, from 1917, the United States).

In general, then, all major powers had to be concerned with political or military developments throughout their region, or even the world. Small powers usually depended for their safety on a single protector or on the ability of their military forces to make any attack on them more costly than would be justified by the benefit of conquering them.

PART I: WHY MODERNIZATION HAS ENDED THE WAR SYSTEM IN WESTERN EUROPE AND WILL EVENTUALLY END IT IN THE WHOLE WORLD

In important parts of the world today, however, the old war system no longer exists. If the British fleet suddenly sank tomorrow, England would be no less safe. Nor would such an event much affect Britain's influence on European affairs. This immense change in the fundamental realities of international relations in Western Europe offers a clue to what we should expect when the whole world becomes modern, as well as to the nature of international relations in the interim.

The war system also gave the great powers reason to try to influence internal changes in other countries. But, unnoticed by most, this issue too has disappeared, like the significance of the British fleet. Recently, for example, the growing power of the Northern Leagues in Italy gave rise to the possibility that Italy might become divided. Eighty years ago there would have been suspicions that foreign agents from rival nations were helping the Northern Leagues in order to weaken Italy—and indeed they might have been. Given the current state of European affairs, however, this possibility did not occur to anyone. No one who had the least grasp of European politics in the 1990s thought that any country cared whether Italy got weaker or stronger. And nobody in Italy had any suspicions that foreign agitators were interfering in Italy's internal affairs. Western Europe had become a "Zone of Peace" in which a country's safety depended on the character of its neighbors, not on military forces and alliances, something that had never existed in the world before.

Western Europe was for millennia as warlike as any part of the globe. But now no nation in Western Europe can imagine attacking or being attacked by neighboring states. Armies and military alliances no longer exert much influence on the relations between the countries of Western Europe, which is no longer divided into competing military blocs. Nobody can say for sure whether there might someday be a war between Western European countries. What is clear today, however, is that the old war system does not apply within Western Europe. No Western European government devotes significant resources to strengthening its military forces in relation to other Western European countries, or to maintaining any alliance or balance of power to protect against potential dangers from Western Europe. (It is true that Britain and France continue to spend a good deal of money maintaining and improving their nuclear forces, but these weapons have nothing to do with a serious calculation of French and British security concerns about their neighbors. Instead, nuclear weapons symbolize the special status Britain and France still claim as victors in World War II. Also, the maintenance of a nuclear deterrent serves as an extra—anachronistic—excuse for not maintaining better conventional forces.)

This description of the fundamental change that has taken place in Western Europe within less than a century doesn't come from political scientists, though most would likely accept it. It comes instead from the situation on the ground; it represents the practical beliefs and behavior of Western European diplomats and politicians. It is not a theory or an ideology or a hope; it is a report on current reality.

Some analysts have argued that the Western European peace that has prevailed since World War II is the result of the American presence in Europe and the need to maintain unity against the Soviet threat. Perhaps these reasons were crucial originally. American military and political presence in Europe made it easier for France and other countries to resist a natural inclination to fear German power. Until about two decades ago, it was very important for prudent Europeans to make sure that the United States stayed in Europe, and not only to deter the Soviet Union. Now things have changed. The disappearance of the Soviet threat hasn't led to an increase in tensions between Western European powers. Few, if any, European leaders, whether they favor more or less American involvement in European affairs, believe today that the relations among Western European countries depend upon United States presence there.

Others argue that the Western European peace is the result of the international institutions that have now evolved into the European Union. France, Britain, and Germany can no longer fight with each other, it is said, because they are bound together in the European Union, with obligations to each other, and with a deep experience of mutual cooperation and discussion of differences in a thousand EU committee and council meetings. Perhaps this is so. But it can also be argued that the EU depends on the peace within Western Europe as much as that peace depends on the EU. Consider a thought experiment: would the disappearance of the EU seriously increase the possibility of war between Western European countries? Not likely.

Western European diplomats talk a lot about the importance of the United Nations, and often insist that the UN is the only source of international legitimacy. Yet few would argue that it is the UN that has made the Western European peace possible. No European diplomat, however sympathetic to the UN, would let the safety of her country depend on the UN if she had any worries about dangers from other Western European countries. The Western Europeans support the UN not to protect their safety, but because they already feel safe from one another. In brief, the Western European peace is not the result of international institutions but of the changed character of all of the countries of the region.

Many in Europe believe that the essential requirement for keeping peace is the suppression or elimination of nationalism, especially in Germany. This theory is one of the primary motivations for devotion to the European Union and to the euro as a replacement for national currencies. Although some Europeans think of themselves as Europeans rather than as French or German or Italian, they are only an important minority, and are far from typical. National loyalties and identification continue to be strong. But they turn out to be completely compatible with an absence of military competition or threat. While the Europhiles would hate to admit it, there is every reason to believe that the collapse or marginalization of the European Union would not increase Western European countries' fear of each other or bring the war system back to the region.

Even though they may not recognize the reason, Western Europeans understand that the old war system no longer operates in their region, and they have developed a set of values and understandings about international relations appropriate for a Zone of Peace. In the past, Europeans expected that countries' rights could only be reliably protected by force or the threat of force. Western Europeans today, however, act as if they believe that international law governs the conduct of all countries. That is, the way in which Europeans respond to conflicts in the Zones of Turmoil (that is, all areas that are not Zones of Peace) implies that they think the rules they follow among themselves also apply to the whole world. They settle conflicts among themselves by negotiation, through legal proceedings, or through peaceful political maneuvering within European institutions. The threat of military force, or the relative military power of the parties, enters their calculations hardly at all. Of course, relative political power, which is closely related to economic power, plays a role in such calculations. France and Germany carry more weight than Belgium and Denmark, but Belgium and Denmark do not hesitate to challenge the bigger powers, and they get their way in a share of disputes. Today, Europeans generalize from the political instincts that govern their current way of relating to each other. They expect countries in other parts of the world, outside the Zones of Peace, to follow the same recently acquired instincts, not to act in the ways in which Europeans themselves traditionally behaved.

How Modernization Reduces the Role of War

To look at the international effects of modernization, we have to focus on Western Europe because it is the only region where there are a number of modern countries and no country that is not modern. If there is any natural experiment from which to learn about the international effects of modernity, it is Western Europe.

Unfortunately, Western Europe is a very limited sample. It has only a dozen or so substantial countries, all of which are "Western." It has only been mostly or entirely modern for a generation or so. It is only recently removed from the experience of World War II and the Cold War. To the extent that it is still in the shadow of its pre-modern experiences, Western Europe may not exemplify the real character of international relations among modern countries over the long-term. But it is all we have to go on, so we will look at it closely.

The principal question is this: is the "deep peace" we observe in Western Europe intrinsically connected to modernization, that is, to the basic changes in the nature of human life that occur once a country (or, in this case, a region) becomes modern? If so, can we expect that war systems will also disappear in other regions as they, too, become modern?

The basic effects of modernity that have influence on international relations are:

1. Modern wealth cannot be achieved by conquest, because it comes primarily from human freedom and creativity.
2. Modern people's lives are based on law and negotiation, and they have little experience with violence or the use of violence to solve problems.
3. In modern countries, political matters are handled by some form of democratic politics.
4. Human life is very valuable in modern societies. People have smaller families (generally only one son) and do not want to put them at risk. People are also used to comfort and order, and they are reluctant to give them up.
5. As war becomes more and more rare, there will be a dramatic reduction in people's expectations about war, making war less of a part of normal thinking. That is, modern conditions will cause war to atrophy.

Most importantly, modernization reduces the role of war because economic growth, not territorial expansion, is the royal road to increased national power and well-being. Adventurism, of whatever kind, no longer works, but any country can raise its national standing and influence by improving its productivity and wealth.

To see that economic growth is the best path to increased national power, we can look at those countries that are pursuing a different approach. The international policies of Venezuela and Cuba, for example, have been largely ideological. When Fidel Castro came to power, Cuba was one of the leading countries of Latin America; today it is among the poorest, and many of its citizens have emigrated. On the other hand, Cuba has had some notable successes in Latin American politics and is extraordinarily influential for its size at the UN. The Castros have had a great run for their money, but the Cuban people could have done much better for themselves pursuing a less ambitious and more conventional policy. Venezuela's Hugo Chavez has been able to use oil money and alliance with Cuba, China, and revolutionary Iran to secure power and influence in Latin America for Venezuela. It is very unlikely, however, that twenty or thirty years from now Venezuela will be better off from Chavez's policies than it would have been if it had just used its natural assets to increase the productivity of its people. Because of the vast quantities of heavy oil in Venezuela, much money will be invested in that country as soon as its political situation makes it reasonable for foreigners to invest there.[2]

Russia is sacrificing productivity growth to pursue the ambition of restoring its status as a great power and maintaining control over its former empire. We can count on the failure of this effort. The Russian example will not lead countries to think that there is a better path to greatness than increasing productivity and wealth.

Iran was the great example of a country that sought to achieve regional and world power by using political and ideological means (including subversion and terrorism) rather than through economic development. But the Iranian approach under Khomeini and his successors was eventually rejected by Iran, although the revolutionary regime still holds power through its bayonets. Young leaders in the coming generation will not be convinced by Iran's experience that there is a better way for their country to get ahead than by becoming as productive as possible.

Countries that want to enhance their standing in the world will not follow the example of Venezuela, Cuba, Russia, or Iran. Small and medium-size countries will instead look to South Korea, Taiwan, and Singapore, while larger countries will look to Japan, China, Brazil, and India. The success and influence of these countries has little or nothing to do with military strength.

Is there any measure of success for a premodern country other than moving to modernity by increasing productivity and wealth? Religious countries could value loyalty to the faith and its commandments as the highest good. There are no countries, however, in which the people and government are saying that they are proud and satisfied because they have maintained their religion even though it handicapped economic development. Religious leaders aren't claiming that their religion is incompatible with increased productivity but worth the sacrifice. Radical Islam is a special case, which I discuss in chapter 5.

Nor do we see countries declaring their pride and satisfaction with maintaining traditional ways of living by resisting the demands of economic growth. In Europe, some countries prefer welfare practices to faster growth, but these are countries that have already become modern and are still growing, albeit slowly.

With respect to international relations, the key thing about pursuing economic growth is that it is primarily an internal matter. No country's economic growth has to come at the expense of other countries. There is no fixed amount of growth that has to be divided among countries. In fact, the opposite is true. Prosperity in one country is usually good for its neighbors. Many kinds of prosperity come in clusters. Countries do most of their trade with countries at comparable levels of development. Most businesses seek to be near other successes in their business. The Asian tigers didn't stand in the way of each other's growth. Most of Asia has been growing very well, while most of South America and Africa have done much more poorly. No one would argue that Brazil's recent success is explained by the relative lack of success of some of its neighbors. It is very significant for the long-term prospects of international relations that so many countries are dominated by goals that are not in conflict with the goals of their neighbors.

Of course, there are ways in which the national interests of countries pursuing economic growth are in conflict with the interests of other countries, and these conflicts will be the stuff of ordinary diplomacy, but they are marginal, not central. They don't involve efforts to destroy or weaken other countries. For example, all countries will try to use trade barriers and restrictions to benefit their own businesses. But this has to be done within the framework of open international trade. It is a matter of elbowing within a basically orderly crowd. Countries compete much as companies compete, and in both cases the competitors have more common than conflicting interests. In both cases, too, success almost always belongs to the competitor that improves its own performance the most, not to the one that succeeds in impeding the competition.

One exception to this happy picture may be the interest of oil exporters in producing political conflict that limits or threatens the world supply of oil and thus keeps oil prices high to the disadvantage of oil-importing nations. Some suggest that some of Russian foreign policy, for example, is influenced by the desire to interfere with the stability of Middle Eastern oil supply so that it can sell its own exports at high prices.

The fact that modern wealth is achieved by innovation and cooperation eliminates some of the biggest incentives to war. The more modern a country becomes, the less it can increase in strength and power by acquiring more territory or population, or by coercing another country.

Modern countries have great difficulty incorporating territories with different populations. Imperial government isn't acceptable for modern countries. Federal systems can work, though they are not easy to organize. We see in modern countries more movement toward breaking into smaller pieces than toward expansion and inclusion. In the United Kingdom, for example, Wales and Scotland are gaining in importance. Even in very centralized France, regional identities such as Normandy or Provence are rising. People in the

Zone of Peace don't have as much instinctive feeling that their safety depends on national unity as they used to, so they feel freer to devote energy to sub-national identities.

Everywhere in the world, as countries become more modern, they increasingly understand that their well-being depends on their effectiveness and cohesion, not on their size. Of the five wealthiest countries, only the United States is large. The United States is a superpower because federalism and American values and traditions make it possible to have a reasonably effective government for a very large and diverse population. India seems to be able to hold an even larger and more diverse population together with federalism and deep-seated values of tolerance and acceptance. Indians still feel that the "idea of India" requires them to hold their whole country together despite the costs of conflict in Kashmir and eastern border areas.

In brief, as the world moves toward becoming modern, incentives for territorial expansion are gradually reduced or eliminated. Of course, emotional or psychological desire for aggrandizement often continues after rational incentives have disappeared (Russia is the outstanding example). But eventually, people's attitudes tend to reflect their interests, and we can already see in the world a gradually declining public appetite for national territorial aggrandizement.

In the modern world, then, the old war system becomes an anachronism because, most obviously, war ceases to serve either an economic or a political function. But there are other reasons as well, deeply rooted in the nature of modern life. First of all, as modernity reduces or eliminates the benefits of war, it also increases the cost of war, because the fundamental effect of modernization is to increase the value of human life and human time. In modern countries, few people have much experience of the death of young people. People don't expect to lose anyone from their small families until they are old. Moreover, wars in the modern world not only fail to make sense economically but they are very costly, especially when you consider that the costs are not limited to the actual time of war. Maintaining a war system is unproductive, and people will be increasingly reluctant to devote their time to sustaining it.

In modern societies, too, most people have little experience of violence, except through forms of entertainment. Violence is not a tool they use to get things done, and rarely are their actions or choices compelled by violence or the threat of violence. The habits and instincts of violence—which perhaps can be found in organized crime, and to a lesser degree among those whose business is fighting crime—are simply not acquired in mainstream modern societies. Such behavior and thinking seem improper and alien.

Having eliminated violence as a means of obtaining objectives, Western Europeans, in their Zone of Peace, are strongly committed to living lawful lives. People believe that the organizations they work for, and especially their government, must be governed by law. There may be more or less devotion to fine points of the law, such as assiduously paying taxes, but there is a sense that law is the essential frame of the society. It is natural for people who think this way to want to base international behavior on law.

Conflicts in the modern world are not resolved by violence, or threats of violence, but through legal procedures and politics. People in Western European countries assume that governments are influenced by politics and that the only means of getting what they want from governments is through politics. Various forms of politics govern most organizations that people deal with in their lives. There *are* dictatorial organizations in modern life, where the top decides and the bottom has no say, but they are not typical. Most of the organizations that people in Western European societies are involved with in their lives at least pretend to allow freedom of speech and to give consideration to many voices. In other words, when people in modern societies think about how to get things done, they think in terms of some form of politics, and some degree of democracy.

Furthermore, the people in each Western European country know that their feelings about violence, law, and politics are shared by the people and leaders in all the neighboring countries. They know that if any one of these countries were to act in violation of these values and expectations, the other countries of the region would strongly disapprove and possibly take (non-violent) action to punish the perpetrator.

The Western European peace, that is to say, is overdetermined. There are many fundamental reasons that there should be a deep peace, all of which explain the results that we see. No special set of temporary factors, or unusual group of current leaders, have come together by chance to produce the current peace. Nor does the peace rest mostly on intellectual or political fashions that could easily change in the course of time. It is possible that someday the romance of war and military heroism will again capture the public imagination. But the current peace is not based solely, or primarily, on current intellectual fashions. If and when new contradictory fashions come to take hold, they will not be enough to overcome the basic structural supports for the peace of Western Europe.

We should not idealize the concept that areas like Western Europe are Zones of Peace. They are not occupied by a new kind of person, made moral and peaceful by modernity, or by a new kind of diplomat making sure that his country must act like a good international citizen in pursuit of justice. Nor will new or improved international institutions be available to maintain international order and justice. The countries of the Zone of Peace will have many conflicts. Diplomats will still pursue their national interests, eschewing truth and fairness whenever necessary to improve relationships and increase their ability to get international support. Non-warlike behavior and expectations will be the result not of increased wisdom or morality but of changed conditions and incentives. International relations, like domestic policy, will continue to operate primarily on the basis of power—not reason, or fairness, or love, or generosity. There will continue to be many forms of power. Nonetheless, military power will continue to decline in importance, from its formerly primary role, becoming eventually largely irrelevant.

We are now living in a transitional period, between the old traditional world and the new modern world. The reality we see today as we look out at international relations will not be the reality of the future. Once the entire world is modern, there will be no war system, even though the character of people and diplomats will not have improved.

Why do I use the weasel-words no "war system" instead of saying outright that there will be no more war? We cannot be sure that there will not be some set of circumstances that produce a war sometime in the centuries after the world becomes modern. We can show that countries will not have rational incentives to go to war, and that armies are not likely to be available, and that there will be many forces working against war, but no one can be sure that no country will ever go to war. Even if armies are mostly or completely discarded, they can be rebuilt, from scratch if necessary.

Nor am I we saying that there will be no terrorism in the modern world. The modern world is not heaven; maybe it will have terrorism. It is almost certain to have crime, including violent crime. But crime and terrorism are not war. When a Rolls-Royce of a world largely without war is given to you, maybe you shouldn't complain that the ashtrays aren't clean. Whatever else is going on, a world without a war system is very different from a world with a war system, which was the only kind of world that was known until now.

The main thesis of this book is that the modern world will be fundamentally different from the worlds of the past. This will be true if the war system is eliminated and war or potential war is not part of the ordinary life of nations and people, and it will remain true even if wars are waged somewhere in the world every fifty or hundred years. It would be nice if there were no wars at all in the coming modern world, and that may be true, but it does not need to be true to prove my thesis about the fundamental difference between the modern world and the past world. To challenge this picture, someone must show not that there might be a war, but that a war could lead much of the world (not only a particular region) to decide that military preparations had become necessary for national security (and not only for a limited time).

What Is the "War System" and Why Will It Disappear?

The war system is any pattern of conditions in the world in which countries normally believe either that they have to have military forces (or alliances, or other outside protectors) to be safe from attack or compulsion, or that military strength will advance their national interest and increase their international influence. The war system makes war, preparations for war, and potential war central elements of human life and of politics and international relations. While there is a war system in place, there will likely be wars.

Most countries, at least in recent years, have kept military forces for defensive reasons. That is, many countries are armed, but few have aggressive intentions. In many cases, it is felt that vulnerability is a provocation. Prudence seems to require that if a country wants to be safe from conquest, domination, or compulsion, it should be capable of protecting itself. It is even possible that sometimes *all* countries maintain their military for defensive reasons. If two countries are suspicious of each other—because of ethnic enmity, differing ideologies, or whatever—each can maintain forces for defensive reasons, and there does not have to be any country with aggressive intentions. The classic prudent principle has been that countries should act on the basis of a potential enemy's capabilities, not its intentions.

Given that we start with an armed world, and that the war system has existed as long as there have been states, what could end the war system?

The war system disappears from any region when the countries in that region feel no danger, or potential danger, of military attack or military threats from others in the region. The war system exists when countries do not feel safe without an army; it goes away when countries feel safe for reasons other than the existence of their army, and know they would feel safe, and not lose their international position, if they gave up their army.

Any country that for many years has prudent confidence that it faces no danger of attack or military pressure, whether or not it has military forces, is likely to decide not to pay the costs of maintaining those forces. Why pay for an army if there is no danger for it to protect against and it doesn't increase influence? A few countries, such as the United States, may have reasons other than the need to defend themselves to keep military forces as long as there are non-modern countries in the world, but generally countries will choose to save their money.

Countries will feel safe if they are convinced that no country close enough to attack would think of doing so. This is true today in the Zones of Peace. Belgium does not think that France would attack in any circumstances, so Belgium does not need even enough of an army to make a French attack a little difficult.

Countries will also feel safe if they believe that the current political conditions are such that any country that thought of attacking would expect to reap so much trouble from the rest of the world—and maybe its own citizenry—that it could not afford to attack. That is, any potential aggressor would be deterred by high diplomatic costs. It's true that unrealistic judgments are often made about the power of "world opinion" and its deterrent value. But there are situations in which diplomatic costs (international opinion reflected in governmental policies) are real, and they can be assessed as realistically as military power. If properly assessed, diplomatic consequences are a legitimate and realistic basis for national security planning.

Some questions remain. No one is going to argue against the proposition that so long as the world is the way it is today, Denmark doesn't have to worry about aggression from Germany or any of its other neighbors in its Zone of Peace. But is this a law of politics that is going to remain true into the indefinite future? Can we be confident that this situation won't change?

The world is much bigger and more diverse than Western Europe, and will never be as cohesive in its entirety as Western Europe is. So the world should not be expected ever to have the kind of community feeling that exists in Western Europe. Japan is not likely to enjoy the kind of relationship with, say, Brazil as the countries of Western Europe have with each other. But other factors will add to the feeling of safety. There will be no Zones of Turmoil, consisting of pre-modern countries (as we have today). Also, the Zone of Peace experience will cover much more territory and will have operated for many more years.

The fundamental reasons for safety, which result from the nature of modern societies, will apply to the whole world, as they apply to Western Europe today. Why shouldn't these factors work as they do in Western Europe now? Why shouldn't countries, after years of experience with the way the modern world works, feel increasingly safe from military threats?

To think about this seriously, one has to wrench oneself out of the present, out of the transitional period we inhabit. Our world contains many non-modern countries, many of them poor and some of them belligerent. Instead, we should imagine the whole world filled with nothing but Swedens and Japans and Americas and Germanies.

Generally armies don't cause war; war and the threat of war cause armies. Armies are essential to the war system, however, and armies make it easier for war to start. As the war system goes away, there will be fewer and smaller armies. The reduction in military forces will make it easier for countries to feel safer, once there are no longer any aggressors around, and will speed and intensify the end of the war system.

The feeling of safety comes first. As we have seen, it will be based on hard-headed analysis of political realities and on the incentives that influence countries' decisions. We see in Western Europe that countries can feel safe even though their neighbors are armed, some even with nuclear weapons. There is no need for a campaign urging disarmament to enable countries to feel safe. The feeling of safety comes before the disarmament. When politicians and publics and diplomats feel safe regardless of military forces, as they do in Western Europe, then eventually military forces will be reduced. Most of them will atrophy into nearly empty shells even before they are officially reduced or eliminated.

When the all-modern world comes, we should expect that it will be as filled with conflict, and as dominated by the pursuit of power, as is the world today. Quite probably, although not necessarily, we can expect that it will be a world of many sovereign states as well as many international institutions. In that modern world, however, the war system that has existed as long as there have been states will no longer exist. War, preparations for war, and the military dimension of national security, will not be part of ordinary life or of people's thoughts and expectations. International conflict, and aggressive instincts, will be expressed by other means than the threat or use of military force, just as in domestic life aggression and conflict are expressed largely non-violently.

PART II: THE PERIOD BEFORE THE WAR SYSTEM ENDS (TWENTY-FIRST CENTURY), AND CHALLENGES TO THE THESIS THAT IT WILL END

We are a long way away from a world populated entirely by modern countries. How will modernization affect international relations in the rest of this century?

The first point is that the world has to be divided into two parts to think about international relations. Zones of Peace (ZOP) and Zones of Turmoil (ZOTs) are fundamentally different. In most of the world, which is now a ZOT, the war system and traditional international relations continue to be in place. Changing economics and military technology, as well as political developments and altered expectations are having an impact on international relations all over the world. Outside the ZOP, however, most of the fundamental traditional wisdom of how countries behave and relate to each other still applies. In the ZOP, on the other hand, the war system no longer exists, and so the fundamental features of how countries relate to each other are different from what they were in the past.

One of the basic features of world politics for the next few generations will be the gradual movement by which regions change from a ZOT to a ZOP. This change is not a matter of individual countries, but of regions, because a country cannot act as if it is in a ZOP unless *all* of its neighbors have become modern democracies.

Central Europe might join the Western European ZOP quite soon. Indeed, the Western European ZOP already includes at least Poland, the Czech Republic, and Austria. Western Europe feels no need to arm itself against these countries, and they feel no military threat from Western Europe, not even from Germany. Of course, Poland still has to take into account potential threats from the east. A country on the outer edge of a ZOP is in a special situation. Our confidence that Poland is no threat to Western European countries is not based on Poland's being a fully modern country, but on the political context of Western Europe—as well as on perceptions of Poland's changing character.

The pattern of the transition to the modern world will not be characterized only by sudden jumps, as whole regions become new ZOPs. Around the world, countries are at various stages of the path to modernity, and they are moving at different speeds and in different ways. A basic feature of the transitional period is that there is no static balance between pre-modern and modern. The amount of modernity in the world will be steadily increasing, though there may well be setbacks along the way.

Long before countries become modern, most will recognize that the golden path to national power is economic growth. They will not be tempted to get ahead by using military power or threats, or by trying to inhibit their neighbors by other means.

Countries will also develop an internal commitment to a society based on law well before they become fully modern, because that is one of the prerequisites of modernization. This is also true with respect to the great reduction in the role of violence and the expectation that politics and negotiation are the sources of decision, rather than arbitrary rule from above. So the basic features of modernity that eventually lead to the elimination of the war system begin to influence regional relationships before all the countries of a region are modern.

Today, in the Zones of Turmoil, where the war system is very much alive, the underlying gradual movement toward the politics of modern democracies is less visible than the various conflicts: Arabs and Muslims against Israel, India against Pakistan, China against Taiwan, Russia against the United States, and Islamists against the West. These current issues are not the subject of this book, though I discuss the most pressing problem, Jihad and Islamism, in chapter 5. Here it is enough to ask, What will happen after the current challenges go away, as all military challenges in the past eventually have?

In the past, the challenges that were overcome were always replaced by new challenges. We are used to international relations being dominated by one kind of clash after another: The rise of nationalism and the destruction of empires; the challenge of nazism and fascism; the spread of communism; Islam's reaction to Western success. The assumption is that there will always be another challenge, that the nature of international relations involves fundamental conflicts with military implications. (This is the assumption that drives Samuel Huntington's famous book *The Clash of Civilizations*.) In thinking about international relations in the coming century, I believe this assumption is wrong. After the current challenges are met, the world may well run out of fundamental challenges requiring countries like the United States to face military rivals.

The Rise of China and India

China is likely to become modern and democratic before it is wealthy enough to equal U.S. military power. Until China becomes wealthy, it is likely to continue to understand that its main need is economic growth, which is greatly helped by international trade and a fairly peaceful world. But this strategy of giving priority to internal development doesn't prevent a large effort to increase Chinese military capability and active diplomatic programs to expand Chinese power and influence. Some Chinese leaders may think that once the country has succeeded in growing wealthy, it could use other, perhaps even violent, measures to make sure it assumes its proper place in the world power structure. But that is not likely to become a major threat because the leaders who have communist assumptions about power are not likely to last that long.

A number of people see military threats in the economic growth of India and China, even if China becomes democratic. (Some of these fears are based on sheer population. According to the most plausible population estimates, at the end of the twenty-first century China will have a population of 850 million people, India of 1 billion people, and the United States of 500 million people, in a world of 7 or 8 billion people.) While China and India are likely to still be behind the United States in per capita income, they are catching up and are likely to surpass the United States in total national product. They will be modern democratic countries.

Is there any reason the United States should be disturbed that China and India are catching up in average wealth or that their total economies may become twice as large as America's? The United States has not gotten much economic benefit from being the largest economy in the world, except for the advantage it has had because of the dominance of the dollar—which would not likely continue to be the primary reserve currency once there are other, larger economies. There is no economic reason to fear Chinese or Indian success. They will face the same kind of domestic political factors that have limited the United States's ability to follow aggressive economic policies while it is the largest power.

On a more personal level, how would Americans feel about ceasing to have the world's largest economy? There will be some popular sense of loss and decline, especially if part of the reason is poor U.S. performance. Undoubtedly, many Americans will, for various reasons, make a big thing of America's "failure to keep up," and it may be at the center of public debate for a generation or so. There will also be strong political pressure on the United States government to try to prevent the United States from being passed by the great Asian powers.

While not denying the strength of national chauvinism among Americans, I think the cynical view of how strongly Americans will resist becoming "number two" and then "number three" is wrong. America's unique economic power has entailed responsibilities, and Americans tend to take pride in how their country has shouldered its obligations—for example, by twice rescuing Europe from tyranny, even though the United States acted, as do most good citizens, somewhat reluctantly. Nonetheless, the main element of American self-esteem does not come from foreign policy or international comparisons but from the character of American domestic society: the quality of life, the feeling of progress, and especially the pleasure of freedom and opportunity for all. So Americans, mostly, will not be devastated by seeing other countries becoming more like America, with China and India achieving larger economies because they have larger populations. Since it will be a slow process, Americans will have plenty of time to adjust to the idea.

The principal reason for confidence that America will eventually accept reduced status is that there will be no good alternative. There will be no reasonable policies available that could prevent China and India from passing the United States In the end, America's social wisdom will probably lead to the conclusion that it is good, and good for America, that other countries achieve the kind of wealth and freedom that America has achieved.

One of the attractive features of the modern world is that the underlying realities make it sensible for the United States to be comfortable with other modern countries achieving larger economies than that of the United States. In the premodern world, when one country changed its relative position by becoming richer, other countries had realistic grounds for concern, and national security had to be recalculated. In an all-modern world, this will not be true.

When China's and India's economies become comparable to that of the United States, they will be capable of building military forces comparable to America's. The question is whether the three giants will indeed build armies to match each other and at what level. Will national rivalries be such that there will be standard three-party maneuvering, with two trying to ally against the third, and the third perhaps trying to ally with smaller powers to compensate? More important, if these rivalries develop beyond the general level of rivalries around the world, will they include competitive military programs? We cannot entirely rely on the experience of Western Europe to predict how the biggest fish will feel about the other biggest fish; maybe traditional competitiveness will last longer among the giants than it has among France, Germany, and Britain, though the characters of Germany and Britain and France were partly formed when they were the giants.

When China first becomes a democracy, it is likely that the United States and China will have large military forces, partly designed against each other. What will happen to those forces in future years? Probably at first, nothing much. Budget pressures in each country will cause a slow erosion. China would have a new government; the shift from communist to democratic might go through several stages, but at some point there may well be a shift to a regime that is clearly a full democracy and a break from previous regimes. The new Chinese regimes might or might not regard previous Chinese military buildups as defensive, and they might or might not view the United States as a benign force in world affairs. Certainly there is a reasonable prospect that a post-communist, democratic government of China would be distinctly nationalistic and proudly Chinese. They might well feel that for China to hold its own in international political jockeying for prestige and influence, the country should not allow the United States to be perceived as having a decisive military superiority. Presumably the United States would welcome the new Chinese government and express its expectation of living in peace and good relations with democratic China. (We are already partly acting that way even before it is called for.) No matter how friendly the two powers are, they will have to treat each other with wariness and they will inevitably have many small disputes to settle.

In this situation, it seems very likely that the United States and China would formally or informally work out agreements for gradual parallel force reductions, primarily as a way of saving money without losing relative position. In other words, at first the balance of military forces would be thought to have some political significance, even though both countries were confident that there was no significant risk of war.

In the following decade or so, it is likely that both the United States and China would substantially reduce their military forces. How far would depend on how much military force had been built up, and whether there were other substantial military powers in the world. China's transition might well happen in the next decade or two, and at the time there might still be developing countries such as Nigeria and Pakistan that are large enough to be dangerous.

All the countries the United States considers threats today are countries that have not yet become modern countries and are not democracies. Gradually these countries will become modern and cease to be threats. However, if they become more productive and competent before they become democratic, they could become more dangerous before they stop being threats.

The most important point is that no country loses because another country grows. Economic growth is not a zero-sum game. Each country's income and influence depends on its own productivity. The world's total product and product per capita has been increasing for two hundred years. There is no reason it cannot keep on increasing for another two hundred years. If there is no limit on the total income, there is no reason for one country's gain to reduce another's. There are no natural resources that are valuable enough to justify a war. Resources will be allocated by price. Every country will be able to buy as much as it can afford.

The common fear—which has roots in the experience of the rise of Prussia and Germany—that the rise of China and India will inevitably cause great conflict, or at least impose major strains on international peace, is anachronistic. This fear is based on a failure to recognize the difference between modern countries and traditional countries, the difference between the conditions of modern parts of the world and the conditions of the past.

As the world becomes modern, the military challenges like those that today shape international relations will gradually (or suddenly) cease to seem important. Maybe there will be one more, or two. But the supply is petering out. Beginning in a generation or two, we should expect that the United States and other great democracies will not be facing any major potential military enemy. Military rivalries or confrontations will be more and more rare or local.

Challenges and Potential Exceptions to the Peacefulness of the All-Modern World

Many of the most serious and informed thinkers about security issues find it very difficult to believe that the war system will ever disappear. They have a keen sense of how long it has existed and how deep its roots are. It is often thought to be an inevitable result of human nature, of the natural aggression of mankind.

We do not expect that this element of human nature is going to change. But much more of life is lived in domestic affairs than in international, and in domestic affairs the role of violence and physical power has been decisively reduced without changing human nature. The same thing can happen in international relations.

The continuing aggressiveness of national leaders and publics will have to contend with changing incentives and realities. In Russia, especially in the 1990s, rival businessmen had each other killed, and killed people who resisted their demands for concessions. In most of the world, we don't do things that way, though human nature is not different elsewhere than it is in Russia. We don't have to ask whether high-powered corporate leaders in America would like to kill their rivals, or union leaders, or "reformers," or others who get in their way. Maybe some consider doing so and recognize how hard it would be to get away with it, and how little good it would do for them. Most of them, even though they are very aggressive and competitive, don't even think of killing or physically threatening those who thwart them. Their nature is not different, but it expresses itself in the vocabulary of their environment and within the patterns of behavior and incentive structure of their society. The human nature of national leaders will be constrained in the same ways, even though they have even more power than the heads of General Electric or Goldman Sachs.

Modern governments will feel safe without armies, but it will always be possible to "reinvent" or resurrect war. Imagine a charismatic and ambitious young leader of some country in some part of a peaceful world of a future century who believes that he (or she) and his country deserve to control more of the world, or that his ideology can improve the world if other nations can be induced to follow his leadership. Such a leader, who becomes convinced that he could not achieve his goals by purely peaceful means, might think that in a mostly disarmed world, a relatively small amount of military power could go a long way. Let's suppose he builds up his country's military force over a period of years, and no one notices (after all, people in an all-modern world no longer worry about military threats). So this ambitious leader might fairly easily put himself in a position in which his army could march, with no effective opposition, and seize the capitals of any or all of his neighboring countries. Or he could use nuclear or biological weapons to threaten great harm to these capitals. Since few political leaders like to have their capitals occupied or destroyed, our hypothetical aggressor might convince some of his neighbors that the better part of valor would be to accept his demands without admitting that they were yielding to a military threat, and without requiring that his army actually march. Such a charismatic leader might go quite far before there began to be an effective response in more distant countries.

Neither the aggressor's nor the victims' conduct is completely incompatible with democracy. We can hope that most democracies would act differently, but we cannot go so far as to claim that such conduct is unimaginable. It could all be done with very modern rhetoric and style. There would not be an occupation, just a "Finlandization" in which the dominated country would understand that it had to do what it was commanded by its aggressive neighbor. Even if there was not much benefit to be gained by the power to coerce the victim countries, the aggressor might think he had done well because of the gratification of his ego, or perhaps because he improved his domestic political position,

This hypothetical chain of events could be the beginning of a return of the war system. At that point, there would be two possibilities. First, either other countries will find diplomatic, political, or economic means to halt the aggression, or the leader's ambitions would be sated. If the latter, there are many ways such a successful use (or threat) of military power could eventually be absorbed in the international system as an episode that does not have any long-time influence on behavior, perhaps after the ambitious leader died. On the other hand, it is possible that other countries would eventually recognize what was happening and decide to build a military force to match the aggressor's. This would take some years to do, whether the response was with a conventional army or with weapons of mass destruction. But once the building of counter forces began, the beginnings of a war system would have returned to at least part of the modern world. But it would not necessarily go far. That would depend on whether countries in a number of regions of the world believed there was a real danger that they would also face military threats and therefore they had to either rebuild military forces or find armed allies. It would be a long way back to a war system, however, and it is not clear why these ideas would spread.

There are other ways one can imagine war coming to the modern world, starting with terrorism, the cause of recent wars. Perhaps terrorists could exist in, and operate from, a modern country against the will of the government. It does not seem likely, as modern countries normally control their territory, but perhaps a terrorist organization could survive and operate clandestinely. If a terrorist group in modern democratic Argentina began killing people in modern democratic Brazil, one can conceive of Brazil's eventually becoming so dissatisfied with Argentina's anti-terrorism measures that it would be ready to go to war with Argentina. But what would be the war aims? To change Argentina's anti-terrorism policy? Not promising. Brazil might decide to try self-help, sending Brazilian troops into the areas where it believed the terrorists were based. Argentina might feel compelled to insist that Brazil remove its troops and, if Brazil did not comply quickly enough, to take some military action against Brazil. This is a barely plausible scenario of war in the modern world; such a scenario would be a deviation from the norm, not the kind of thing that would lead to the world becoming more warlike.

Let's try something else. Suppose that Brazil had become very arrogant. While Argentina and Brazil's other neighbors had become as rich as France is now, Brazil had become twice as rich. And suppose that Brazil's Spanish-speaking neighbors were all resentful of Brazil, and that they deliberately discriminated against Brazil in the South American regional organizations and in the United Nations, automatically opposing whatever Brazil proposed. Brazil might have come to think of itself as better than its neighbors, as well as stronger, and entitled to deference, whereas it was getting only insults and resentment. In this situation, Brazil's actions against Argentinian terrorists might be part of a policy of letting its neighbors know that they would have to pay more respect to Brazil. In this case, Argentina would have more reason to use military force to respond to the Brazilian attack, and Brazil's other neighbors might be inclined to help Argentina. One can imagine this scenario slowly developing over a decade or so, with a series of relatively small incidents. During this time, each of the countries might have gradually built up their military forces while thinking and saying to themselves that war was impossible.

If this pattern doesn't develop over the Spanish-Portuguese divide in South America, it might develop over the divide between the United States and everyone else, or between India and China or Pakistan, or between Russia and its neighbors, or between Nigeria and its neighbors. It might happen three or four generations after the last war, when memory of the horrors of war had become weak, and perhaps there had been an artistic fashion of glorifying heroism, courage, self-sacrifice, and national pride. Or willingness to use military force might arise on the basis of ideology. Some countries might think that their form of democracy is different enough from other countries' form of democracy to be worth fighting over. Such a country might, for example, seek independence from an international organization it thought was violating its principles, and the organization might seek to compel it to remain in the fold.

All of these scenarios are probably possible. That is, we cannot have enough confidence in what we can know about the character of modern countries to assert that these scenarios violate the nature of what that world will be like in all its variations over many centuries. According to the conception of modernity described here, however, these possibilities do not represent the normal course of events or expectations that will shape national policies and international relations. If they happen, they will be seen as aberrations, and will not bring a return of the war system.

NOTES

1. Winston Churchill, *The World Crisis* (London: Scribner's, 1923), vol. 1, p. 123.

2. Venezuela has very large deposits of a form of oil that requires a lot of expensive processing before it can be used. Until recently this oil was too

expensive to compete but now it could make Venezuela one of the three or four largest oil exporters in the world, while creating economic development in Venezuela because of the industry necessary for processing the oil. But this cannot happen until there is a government in Venezuela in which it is reasonable for investors to have enough confidence to justify billions of dollars of fixed investment.

5

THE JIHADI CHALLENGE AND ISLAM IN THE FUTURE

People look at what's happening in the Muslim world today, especially the Arab part of that world, and doubt that modernization will spread through the world in this century, or even the next. Maybe the clash of civilizations will prevent the spread of zones of peace. Maybe Muslims will gain control of Europe, setting back the expansion of modernity. Maybe Islam will prevent Muslim nations, or at least the Arabs, from modernizing.

The future impact of Islam on the world hinges on the outcome of a struggle within Islam itself, between modernizers and anti-Western fundamentalists (the Iranian revolutionaries of 1979, the Wahhabi ideologues, the Muslim Brotherhood, al-Qaida militants today, and others like them). The most important "modernizers" are not leaders or thinkers trying to modernize Islam. They are the mass of ordinary Muslims, who are deeply attached to their Muslim identity and also are attracted to features of modern life, especially affluence and freedom. They are not trying to modernize Islam; they just want some of what they see on television while continuing to fast during Ramadan and to feel that they are part of Islam.

The fundamentalists, in the words of Bernard Lewis, "feel that the troubles of the Muslim world at the present time are the result not of insufficient modernization but of excessive modernization." They wish to return to what they call "true Islam," to reject infidel imports, and to restore Sharia (Muslim law). According to the fundamentalists, who are now the most visible and important Islamic leaders but who do not represent a majority of Muslims, modernity is in unavoidable conflict with Islam: the "modern" is intrusive, decadent Westernization and poses a fatal threat to Islamic values.[1] Muslim rage, writes Lewis, is directed

> against the whole process of change that has taken place in the Islamic world in the past century or more and has transformed the political, economic, social, and even cultural structures of Muslim countries. Islamic fundamentalism has given an aim and a form to the otherwise aimless and formless resentment and anger of the Muslim masses at the forces that have undermined their traditional values and loyalties and, in the final analysis, robbed them of their beliefs, their aspirations, their dignity, and, to an increasing extent, even their livelihood.[2]

The future we are concerned with will be determined by the behavior of the masses of Muslim individuals. Some of the time they will act individually on the basis of thoughtful concern about the lives of their families and about the obligations of their faith. At other times they will act as part of Muslim crowds, vulnerable to emotional appeals. Over time, all kinds of Muslim behavior in each country will accumulate to determine that country's choice about the direction of that part of the Muslim world. Each country's choice will influence other countries and individuals throughout the Muslim world.

ECONOMIC MODERNIZATION

Arab countries today lag far behind the West. Low productivity, low job creation, and high birth rates have made for grim forecasts. Israel's per capita GDP, for example, is more than five times that of Jordan, though in 1948 they were essentially even. Modern communications, meanwhile, have made these inequalities painfully apparent to those Arabs who lag behind. They deem "globalization" as thinly disguised American economic exploitation.

The difficulties are substantial, and we cannot predict exactly how or when they will be overcome. But we can be confident that these very real difficulties are not sufficient to keep Islamic societies permanently off the path that the rest of the world is treading. Countries like Turkey, Tunisia, Lebanon, and Malaysia demonstrate that Islam does not necessarily impede the national learning that is economic development.

Whatever the theoretical frictions between Islam and modernization, a large number of Muslims, including many who are fully practicing and committed, are able to become modern. Vali Nasr of the Fletcher School argues that "the Dubai effect"— that is, free trade, access to foreign markets, and middle-class commercialism—will liberalize the Middle East even as it preserves a healthy respect for Islamic tradition.[3] Iran, Iraq, and Indonesia are examples of Muslim countries that are already moving along the path to modernity.

To think about the possibility of the Islamic world's becoming modern, one must consider the various groups of Muslims separately. First are the Muslims who live as minorities in non-Muslim countries—most notably Indian Muslims, who make up about 15 percent of Indians and 10 percent of all Muslims. When India becomes a modern country, most Indian Muslims are likely to be living modern lives and to have values and behavior not too different from other Indians.

Indonesia, the largest Muslim country, with 12.5 percent of all Muslims, is already well on the way to becoming modern. It is possible that Indonesia's Muslim character will prevent it from becoming a modern country during the coming century, but that judgment can't be based on what has happened so far.

A large share of the one percent of Americans who are Muslims, including many who are strongly committed to their religion, are successful in integrating into modern American society. While most of the mosques and the most prominent Muslim organizations seem to be affiliated with the part of Islam that speaks against accommodation between Islam and the West, they do not reflect the actual behavior of the great majority of American Muslims (though a larger share of the younger generation may be more influenced by the radicalism of many of the mosques).

The fundamental point, however, is the difficulty of imagining 85 percent of the world living modern lives for many generations while the Muslim world continues to reject growth. Some Muslims will continue to regard the modern world as corrupt and Godless, but experience suggests that for the majority of Muslims this attitude will not withstand the appeal of modern freedoms and economic opportunities. The movement toward modernization will also increase in strength as both lay Muslims and great sheikhs begin to argue that modernity is compatible with traditional Islam and with the example of many million devout and faithful Muslims living modern lives.

Recall that Arabs are only about a quarter of all Muslims. The largest Muslim populations are in Indonesia, Pakistan, India, and Bangladesh. If these Asian Muslims, or even half of them, find ways to accommodate Islam with modernization, live in peace with their neighbors, and become modern countries, it will be very hard for the Arab countries to hold on to a form of Islam that prevents them from also becoming modern.

SOCIOCULTURAL AND POLITICAL RESISTANCE TO MODERNIZATION

There exist in Islam values and ideas that may be hard to change but will change if an Islamic country becomes fully modern. This is not the place for detailed analysis of Islamic—or Arab—cultures, so I will point to a single example: the subjugation of women (forced marriages, polygamy, honor killings, female circumscision, and the wearing of the hijab, niqab, and burqa). For antimodernist, fundamentalist Muslims, Western recognition of women's equality amounts to a form of debauchery. Although it is difficult to determine whether gender equality is a cause or result of development, a large degree of gender equality is universally found in modern countries. Such equality may be expressed differently in different cultures, but it is a characteristic of modernization, and therefore the Islamic world, too, will have to make this and other fundamental and often highly personal changes.

A second sphere of resistance to modernization is political. Islam does not recognize a distinction between the political and religious realms ("Islam is politics or it is nothing," Ayatollah Khomeini once said.) This is why, today, many Islamic countries are more deeply Islamic than Christian countries are Christian. It is also why outside of Turkey and Iraq (so far), Islamic experiments with democracy have failed, and free and representative government, with the guarantee of individual rights, has not taken root. (Those roots in Turkey are now beginning to be tested.) Democracy, based on the rule of the people, grates against the Islamic view that law comes from God. It is regarded as a denial of the sovereignty of God.

My conclusion from all this discussion and history is that it is not impossible that someday Muslims might reconcile democracy and Islam. Although liberal democracy is a product of the West, and the history of Muslim states is without exception one of autocracy, nothing in the nature of Islam makes it impermeable to the development of democratic institutions or the increasing desire for freedom. Bernard Lewis, to cite him again, observes that even though "traditional Islam has no doctrine of human rights," it does have a tradition of emphasis on law, and of rulers being obligated to consult with citizens.

ISLAM AND PEACE

Today, the conflicts between Muslims and non-Muslims, and various conflicts within the Muslim world, make it hard to believe that peace is imminent. (This is certainly not to say that Islam as a religion is necessarily a source of conflict in the world.) This prompts two questions:

(1) What are the prospects for jihad?
(2) Will a major part of Western Europe come to be dominated by Muslims, and, if so, what will that mean for European modernity?

To think clearly about the long-term prospects for jihad, or any other systematic Muslim war, we need to understand something of Islam's view of itself and its relation to the world. Amidst the rich variety of Islamic schools of thought, two ideas are virtually universal. First is the notion that Allah intends Islam and its law, Sharia, to be accepted by all peoples. A widely accepted implication of this is that, in principle, a permanent state of conflict exists between the Islamic part of the world, *Dar al Islam* ("the House of Islam"), and the rest of the world, which has not yet accepted Islam, *Dar al Harb* ("the House of War"), now led by the United States. (Some Islamic jurists recognize an intermediate *Dar al Sulh*, or "House of Truce," whereby a non-Muslim society is granted a measure of internal autonomy.) The doctrine permits truces of indefinite length, and does not require that the war with infidel nations be actively prosecuted every day. Even so, the idea of Islamization shapes in various ways the attitudes of Muslims toward non-Muslims, especially among Muslims who believe that they must actively wage *Dawa* (missionary) programs to influence unbelievers, or that they must subvert infidel governments—with violence, if necessary. This stark view has not prevented Muslims from living amicably with non-Muslims, and various Islamic thinkers have reconciled the theoretical state of war with a normal absence of war in real life. Nonetheless this basic Islamic view of the world must be weighed when trying to gauge the future of Muslims' relations with themselves and with the outside world.

The second fundamental idea is that jihad—from the Arabic root for "striving" or "struggle"—is one of the basic obligations of Muslims. In mainstream Islamic thought, the primary meaning of "jihad" connotes, and has always connoted, violent battle against infidels. There is a great diversity of Islamic opinion about what circumstances, if any, call for jihad and who has the authority to declare a jihad. But every classic Muslim jurisprudent has discussed jihad at length, and it does not seem plausible that most Muslims in this generation will come to believe that jihad, as a battle against unbelievers, is not an important aspect of Islam.

The world's approximately 1.6 billion Muslims hold to these ideas in diverse ways. Probably less than five percent have a strong religious commitment to violent jihad against the degenerate West. An even smaller group has an *ideological* (that is, not religious) commitment to fighting the West, as Saddam Hussein did and Bashir Assad of Syria does, and use jihadist rhetoric to gain popular Muslim support. Perhaps a third of Muslims have some level of religious antagonism to the West without having any commitment to jihad, and perhaps another ten percent share an ideological antagonism to the United States, "the Great Satan," but do not think in terms of an obligatory state of war. About 15 percent don't hold any attachment to jihad as a practical matter but have strong religious feelings, and in some circumstances they could be impelled by religious imperatives. The largest group of Muslims, amounting to perhaps 40 percent, are not driven in their political thinking and behavior by Islam, though their Muslim identity usually has personal significance. (These numbers are qualitative estimates, not a report on a particular survey or calculation.)

Today, as terror attacks have made painfully clear, a very small but significant part of the Muslim world is trying to foment violent jihad against the West (and against Muslim regimes that reject the call for jihad).[4] A much larger group, but still a small minority, believes that violent jihad is in principle appropriate, but not yet tactically or strategically feasible. Members of this second group do not oppose jihad, but judge that violent jihad cannot at present succeed, or that it would delay the triumph of Islam. In the meantime, such Muslims—the various branches of the Muslim Brotherhood offer the best example—are using mostly non-violent means to work toward the same end. Inasmuch as both groups define themselves by their antagonism toward the West, they cannot be placated or appeased.

The pressing question for the immediate future is whether Osama bin Laden and other violent jihadis can succeed in changing what is still a very small jihad into the much larger one they are trying to promote, by gaining control of one or more major Muslim countries. A secondary question is whether their little jihad, the one we watch in the news today, will be effectively contained or ended. This will depend on the sizable minority of Muslims who are determined to defeat the West and to establish Sharia and a worldwide caliphate and are ready to act on this determination, violently or non-violently. Someday, they or their successors may think differently, but in the short term there is no point in trying to change their minds. Therefore, the only way of preventing a large-scale violent jihad is to continue to act in a way that convinces these jihadis that because the West is so strong, now is not the right time, as the Muslim Brotherhood had been convinced.

Violent jihad has little chance of success against a determined defense unless it has some support or tolerance from at least one Muslim government. The recent trend is that jihadis find bases not by gaining control of a Muslim country but by operating in a failed state, or by making a country ungovernable (as we are now witnessing in Afghanistan, Somalia, Yemen, and parts of Pakistan). In order to prevent terrorists from finding sanctuary, the West, largely represented by the United States, has the difficult task of helping such countries to control their territories.

The jihadis are boxed in by a fatal dilemma. To generate momentum and convince more sympathetic Muslims that jihad can win and has Allah's support, they have to be able to kill large numbers of Americans in the United States; September 11, 2001, cannot be a one-shot achievement, a decade in the past. But if there are several more 9/11s, the United States will mobilize to fight back, and the blind eye now turned to Muslim support for extremist behavior in the United States will be opened.

One mirror of this dilemma is the widespread Arab belief that the Twin Towers were brought down by the CIA or by Israelis, often accompanied by admiration of Osama bin Laden because he delivered righteous retribution for American arrogance.

Another version of this inherent dilemma applies to "peaceful" advancement of Muslim power in Western countries. It is hard for Muslims to get people in democratic countries to accept increased Muslim power without using small-scale strong-arm tactics. A little violence in a non-violent society can be very effective, as organized crime often demonstrates. But too widespread use of violence creates a backlash, a determination to enforce the law against those who are using violence to gain power, as organized crime learns from time to time.

For at least the next decade, and quite possibly for the next several generations or even longer, we can expect that there will be a significant minority of jihadi Muslims making tactical decisions about whether the time is right for violent jihad. During these generations, there will also be a long-term struggle within Islam about the requirements of Islamization, the role and nature of jihad, and the kind and degree of modernization that is compatible with Islam. It seems likely that over time the balance of thinking within the Muslim world is likely to change. Moderate Muslim thinkers who find principles in Muslim law and tradition that allow pious Muslims to accept permanent peaceful accommodation with non-Muslims might find wider acceptance. Some Muslims, who just want to worship, won't care much about what Islam says about jihad. Others may become secular, or adopt a less ideological form of Islam (such as Sufism). The future of jihad is likely to be decided by competition between various components of the Muslim world. As Daniel Pipes argues: "radical Islam is the problem and moderate Islam is the solution."

Non-Muslims cannot usefully participate in the struggle within Islam about the meaning and requirements of Islam. But there is one way the West can have a major influence. Radical Islam needs triumphs over the West to succeed in dominating Islam. Within the Muslim world, the radicals gain advantage when their external policies seem to succeed and when Western powers act as if they are afraid. Deference paid to radical Islamic forces by the democratic great powers helps those forces to dominate the Muslim arenas. Now moderate Islam is weak and defensive. Moderates face the danger of violent reprisals. They seem to be only a small part of the argument within Islam. This is partly the result, as we see clearly in Iran, of the West's letting the radicals have symbolic or real success internationally while withholding recognition and respect from the moderate Muslim voices. The greatest help the West can give to moderate Muslims is to defeat both diplomatic and violent attacks against the West by radical Muslims. The moderates have a chance in the Muslim discussion only when the radicals look like losers.

Meanwhile, there is no conceivable way that Islam can defeat the West by means of a large-scale violent jihad—which would be disastrous for both sides, but much worse for Muslims. The West holds too much military and economic power, regardless of Muslim control of so much oil. Even if a jihad lasted for a generation, and required significant arming by Western democracies, there is no reason to think that it would restore a war system in modern countries. While a large-scale jihad would force Western countries, and maybe all modern countries, to defend themselves, it would not make them more threatening to each other. During and after a jihad, for the reasons discussed in chapter 4, modern countries would not be concerned with launching a war against each other.

The far more likely scenario, however, is that the widespread Muslim rejection of jihad will become ever more pronounced. Muslim voices speaking for less-confrontational Islamic thinking will become less suppressed. Gradually some countries will develop modes of Islamic thinking that are compatible with modernization. Due to their success, these countries will become increasingly attractive to the rest of the Muslim world, and the plausibility of jihad will slowly fade away.

Consider a concrete example of how this might happen even in the short-term. The recent resurgence of radical Islam and jihadi thinking has had two specific causes that activated underlying Muslim fervor. The first was the Islamic revolution initiated by Ayatollah Khomeini in Iran in 1979, which has been actively promoted by the Iranian regime ever since. The second was the roughly $4 billion per year Saudi program to promote Wahhabism— or as they prefer to call it, Salafi Islam. This program, which is funded largely by members of the Saud family, probably not by the government, was to an important degree a Saudi response to Khomeini's bid for dominance of radical Islam. (The radical takeover of the Mecca holy places, which the Saudis were able to overcome only with the help of French forces, happened at about the same time as the Iranian revolution.)

And yet, as of this writing, the Iranian revolutionary regime has been seriously undermined by popular uprisings and by division within the Shiite religious leadership. After that regime falls, probably in this decade, it is not unreasonable to hope that the Saudis can be convinced or compelled to cut back by at least ninety percent the amount of money they spend outside their country to promote their extreme version of Islam. If the two engines that have driven the radicalization of the Muslim world for more than a generation stop running, the Muslim world is likely to begin to look very different from how it looks today. There would be much more room for moderate voices.

ISLAMIZATION BY PEACEFUL MEANS

Apart from jihad, Islam might present another impediment on the path to modernization: some fear that Islam could come to dominate by primarily peaceful means.

Take the case of Europe, which is home to about thirty-eight million Muslims, or about 5 percent of its population. Nearly half of Europe's Muslims are in Russia. The Balkan countries of Kosovo, Albania, and Bosnia have Muslim majorities. Bulgaria, like Russia, is about 12 percent Muslim, and Macedonia one-third. In Eastern Europe, except for the Muslim-majority parts of Russia and the Balkans, there has been no movement toward Muslim domination.

In Western Europe as a whole, the twelve million Muslims account for about 4 percent of the population, most of them immigrants (or children of immigrants) from Turkey, North Africa, and South Asia. Germany, France, and the Netherlands have 5 to 6 percent Muslim minorities, while most other countries in Western Europe have much smaller Muslim populations. Even in Britain, where the mostly Pakistani-origin Muslims have become prominent, Muslims constitute less than 3 percent of the population.

A number of experts believe Western Europe is fated to become controlled by Muslims because of the growing Muslim share of the population, lack of Christian (and secular) interest in defending Western values, and the strong identification European Muslims have with Islam. Some people fear that by mid-century, France,

Germany, and the Netherlands might be dominated by Muslims who see themselves as part of the Muslim world, not as Europeans whose religion is Islam, and that such concentrated Muslim power might set in motion an irreversible process of suppressing, driving away, and converting the non-Muslim population, as has happened in other lands of Muslim conquest.

Here is the scenario for such a result, which I regard as highly unlikely: Muslims use violence and threats, combined with voting power, to gradually impose restrictions on non-Muslim speech and to veto government actions they consider "anti-Islam." This Muslim assertiveness and self-confidence adds to the romantic appeal of Islam for young people and leads to more conversions to Islam from a flaccid and uninspired Christian community. Muslims would increasingly obtain seats in parliaments and ministries, and they would be able to pass increasingly pro-Muslim programs concerning schools, Sharia law, immigration, and foreign policy.

Muslims then exploit their power by securing government favor for Muslim-controlled companies and institutions. The result would be many companies doing a lot of discrimination in favor of Muslims. Some would discriminate because it would help in dealing with the government, or with some customers who want a "Muslim-friendly" label, and others because of Muslim ownership or control of companies. With growing Muslim economic and political power, and a political environment in which Muslims can complain about discrimination against Muslims but non-Muslims are prevented from complaining about discrimination in favor of Muslims (because that is "Islamaphobia"), pro-Muslim discrimination is invited. It is not likely that Muslims would impose the traditional *jizya* poll tax on Christians and Jews (see the Quran IX: 29), but if Muslims can speak against non-Muslims in ways that non-Muslims cannot speak against Muslims, which is already beginning to be true, then a substantial start has been made in giving *dhimmi* (second-class or subordinate) status to non-Muslims.

Some scholars, though I am not one, believe that some version of this scenario may occur over the succeeding generations. What we have seen so far is that the Muslim cause has been pursued by intransigence, threats, and use of violence. Besides the bombings in Madrid (2004) and London (2005), severe ethnic tensions have arisen following both the murder of the Dutch filmmaker Theo van Gogh by Islamic extremists in November 2004 and the Danish publication of the "Muhammad cartoons" in September 2005. In late 2005, there were riots among disaffected Muslims in suburban Paris housing projects. Cultural patterns persist, and some Muslim immigrants (or their children) may be driven toward more fundamentalist versions of Islam. The mainstream Muslim leadership has rejected any interest in adopting European values or in identifying with any European nations. Those who are most familiar with historic and contemporary patterns of behavior and belief in Muslim countries argue that once Muslims gain power in Western Europe, they will move steadily to increase Muslim control and to dominate and suppress the non-Muslim part of the population, which they will treat as *dhimmis*.

It is not impossible that Germany and France, and possibly a few other Western European countries, could be largely controlled by Muslims by the middle of this century, though I believe that it is unlikely to happen. But for Muslims to become a majority in France and Germany by 2050, about sixty million more Muslims would have to immigrate to those two countries in the next forty years— a tripling of the rate up to now, which has held steady at about half a million immigrants a year for France and Germany combined. Despite much higher Muslim fertility it would also require perhaps fifteen million conversions and five million non-Muslims emigrating from France and Germany during the next forty years. So much immigration would result in France and Germany having a combined population of something close to 200 million at mid-century, whereas without increased immigration rates they are expected to have a combined population of some 140 million.

It is very unlikely that Muslims could become a majority in France and Germany by mid-century, but it could happen by 2070 or 2080. In any event, they will have rapidly increasing political power, if they are united, long before they are an actual majority. No matter how many Muslims there are in France and Germany, they will have all the normal political challenges of organizing to make themselves an effective political force. Few groups are able to keep together and to present political programs that serve their interests as they become large and begin to gain power.

Somewhere during the sixty or seventy years before Muslims could realistically become a majority in Western Europe, the character of Islam in Europe may change.[5] After all, by that time many European Muslims will belong to the third and fourth generations born in Europe. Muslim populations in Western Europe have become large only in the last decade or two, and these populations are primarily the first generation of immigrants and their children, who are often more radical than their parents. The great bulk of this population is not assimilating to European norms, beyond asserting their rights to benefits and acceptance. But another pattern is also slowly beginning to be seen: young, educated Muslim professionals and business people are emerging, people who are active in European life with positions attained in conventional ways, mostly by merit. Muslim immigrants and their descendants are likely eventually to absorb elements of the host culture, even if the first and second generations now look almost immune. Increasingly, over many decades, European Muslim political leaders exercising Muslim political power in European government, society, and politics may find that they can do better by adopting, or at least accommodating, European styles and approaches. The process of Islamization of Europe may also be a process of modernization of Islam.

ISLAMIZATION AND MODERNIZATION

Even though Muslim control of important parts of Western Europe may not be likely while Islam is in aggressive mode, the hypothetical possibility may tell us something about the definition and resilience of modernity. The idea that major Western European countries might become Muslim-controlled, no matter how unlikely, raises the question of whether the world could relapse after becoming modern. Could a Muslim-controlled Germany and France still be modern? If not, should such "backsliding" be seen as something that could prevent the whole world from completing the passage to a modern world? Or, alternatively, should we say that a Muslim country in Western Europe illustrates the range of forms that "modern" can take?

The first dimension of the question pertains to the democratic character of an Islamicized European country. Muslim governments might be able to hold power with minimum use of violence. If non-Muslims accept Islamic rule, the governments would not have to install a police state. But such a regime would still not meet our definition of democracy: It would not allow freedom of speech and organization for groups that wished to dissent from Islamic rule.

If Muslims come to power in France and Germany through the use of violence and other non-democratic, illegal measures, the French and German economies would continue to be commercial and urban, based on trade and mental work rather than subsistence agriculture, but productivity and incomes would fall (though it is hard to predict how far). For many years people would continue to live in clean and safe "modern" conditions. Such countries would be "de-modernizing," though for a long time they would only fail to meet the definition of modern countries by not being democratic, by being more violent, and quite possibly by being much more willing to go to war with their neighbors. Muslim-controlled parts of Western Europe would not be a zone of peace where countries had no fear of their neighbors.

There are several reasons to believe that this scenario of Muslim domination is unrealistic. First, so much non-democratic behavior, and such prevalence of violence in ordinary life, would reduce the competitiveness of French and German economies. The Muslims of France and England would face the same temptations and pressures to reenter (or to avoid completely departing from) the modern world as the Muslims of Egypt and Syria. Therefore, they might gradually give up the practices that had inhibited productivity.

Second, the scenario depends on a large share of the population being recent immigrants who had not been subjected to the influences of modern life. The France and Germany of these scenarios would not be countries with almost entirely modern populations. In 2050 such Muslims would not be a people whose lives had little experience of violence, so they would not have had the formative experience that makes a modern country modern and would not necessarily act like a modern country. Thus their non-modern behavior would not contradict the thesis that a successful post-industrial economy is incompatible with tyranny. A population that inherits a modern economy is like one that has a high income from oil; it doesn't necessarily act like a country that earns its modernity.

Third, if there were Muslim control of France and Germany by 2050, there might well be a strong tendency for Muslim behavior to move toward democratic standards, or for a movement against undemocratic Muslim behavior to grow and eventually to woo those countries back to modern democracy. Such a movement would be greatly helped by the democracy of the other European countries. The Muslims would, by that time, be heavily Europeanized, and the two countries would again be modern countries that act like modern countries.

Finally, this example illustrates our general position that the democratic character of modern societies is not an absolute law of nature but an extremely strong tendency. Just as Singapore, uniquely among modern countries, has so far not become democratic, so in the future there may very rarely, or under very unusual circumstances, be modern countries that lose their democracy and no longer act like ordinary modern countries. Although we cannot be certain that all modern countries will always be democratic, we can count on the fact that the overwhelming majority of countries will be democratic almost all of the time because of the inherent conditions of modern life.

Professor Daniel Pipes argues that the danger to the great democracies from peaceful Muslim programs to extend Muslim power in the West may be greater than the danger of jihad. While the peaceful-takeover danger may be greater than the jihad-victory danger, it is still a very small danger. The goal the Muslim extremists proclaim is to install Sharia throughout the world and to create a new caliphate that governs everywhere. The possibility that these goals will be achieved is so small that it can be ignored. Muslims may succeed in reducing the degree to which the United States, for example, protects values such as freedom of speech, separation of church and state, and the equality of women. But a creeping growth of concessions to Muslim abuse of multicultural values, and to Muslim threats of violence, cannot go so far as a subjugation of the country to Muslim law and Muslim courts. Long before Muslims and their non-Muslim supporters come to power in the United States there will be a backlash by the American majority. Although it is possible to imagine that Americans may tolerate the imposition of foreign values on Muslims in the United States—but even that is unlikely to happen on a large scale—it is inconceivable that they would tolerate these values and rules being imposed on non-Muslim Americans, even if Islam had triumphed in most of the world.

Although much of Islam today seems inherently in conflict with modernity, in the long run Islam and modernity are compatible. "Islam," Bernard Lewis remarks, "is one of the world's great religions . . . It has given dignity and meaning to drab and impoverished lives. It has taught people of different races to live in brotherhood and people of different creeds to live side by side in reasonable tolerance. It inspired a great civilization in which others besides Muslims lived creative and useful lives and which, by its achievement, enriched the whole world."[6] Fully modern people can be practicing and faithful Muslims. The doctrines, laws, and history of Islam are protean enough for modern people to be able to find Islamic support for modern values and behavior. There already exist Muslim thinkers and clerics who provide leadership and authority for such Muslim behavior.

One country at a time—or faster—Arabs will insist that groups and rules that stand in the way of moving into the modern world must give way and allow for a new synthesis. This will be true of Islam in general, too. People will find ways to make their Muslim identity compatible with modern life, as have many tens of millions of Muslims already in countries like Turkey, Indonesia, Malaysia, and Morocco. There will also be significant emigration from countries that stay behind until, eventually, a tipping point in the Muslim world will be reached. Perhaps some of the non-Arab Muslim countries will make the change first. Such examples will make it harder for the Arabs to hold out.

This is not a prediction that Islam will disappear, or even that there will be a significant decline in the percentage of people who are Muslim. Today, the strongest part of Islam's conflict with the modern world comes primarily from the fact that a small, backward-looking component of Islam has been able to use immense oil wealth to become the dominant element in the Muslim world, in parallel with the international effects and efforts of revolutionary Iran. Eventually this Wahhabi version of Islam will recede to the minor importance it had fifty years ago, in part because more and more Muslims will come to see how handicapped they are by that version and recognize that other Islamic ways of thinking provide a better alternative. In brief, the nature of Islam will not prevent the Muslim part of the world from becoming modern.

When the whole world is modern, 1.6 billion Muslims will not for very long be satisfied to live pre-modern lives. And when the fully Muslim countries find ways to accept critical modern values, any advanced countries that have become Muslim-dominated are not likely to be far behind, and they might even help to lead the way.

NOTES

1. In the 1990s, the political scientist Samuel P. Huntington famously suggested that the Cold War between the West and Communism would be replaced not by traditional rivalries between nation-states but by a "clash of civilizations" in which "the dominating source of conflict will be cultural" (*The Clash of Civilizations and the Remaking of World Order* [New York: Simon and Schuster, 1996]). In the book I wrote with Aaron Wildavsky, *The REAL World Order* (New Jersey: Chatham House, 1996, 2nd edt.), we dissented from the "clash of civilizations" view on the grounds that the major coming clash, if any, would arise not between Islam and Western or other civilizations, but *within* Islam between those who turn their backs on modernization and fervently wish that Islamic theocracy could once again triumph and those who would like to find a way for Islam to find

accommodation with the rest of the world. Muslim countries will only be able to enter the modern world after the long struggle among Muslims between the two broad forms of Islam has been won by those for whom Islam is compatible with modernization. Islam is an exceptionally diverse product of fourteen centuries of a civilization reaching from Morocco to Indonesia, and of a great many literary and philosophic and legal schools. It contains too great a multitude of beliefs to restrict the possibilities for how Islam will develop in the future.

Other scholars, such as Ephraim Karsh of the University of London, would argue that the aggressive element of Islam today is not primarily a response to Muslim frustration or antipathy to modernity, but an expression of traditional and inherent Islamic ways of responding to the world. While Karsh can make a strong case for this on the basis of Muslim writing and history, it is less clear that the great body of Muslims living today are prepared to act on the Islamic drives that Karsh describes.

2. Bernard Lewis, "The Roots of Muslim Rage," *The Atlantic Monthly* (September 1990).

3. Vali Nasr, *Forces of Fortune: The Rise of the New Muslim Middle Class and What It Will Mean for Our World* (New York: Free Press, 2010).

4. Some Middle East Studies scholars argue that "jihad" means the struggle for self-control and self-improvement, and that any conflict between Muslim groups and the United States is merely a political response to American arrogance and attempts to dominate and control the Middle East. But I take the groups that have been attacking the United States—since well before the United States removed Saddam Hussein from power in Iraq—at their word. They say they are conducting a jihad, holy war, on behalf of Islam and call on all Muslims to join them in this kind of jihad.

5. See Ronald Inglehart, "Muslim Integration into Western Cultures: Between Origins and Destinations," Faculty Research Working Papers Series (Harvard University, John F. Kennedy School of Government: March 2007).

6. Bernard Lewis, "The Roots of Muslim Rage."

II

THE NOT-YET KNOWN

DEMOGRAPHY

How Personal Decisions Will
Shape the World's Future

Just as Beethoven could build a complex and powerful symphony on the base of a simple four-note theme, a few demographic variables echo through our lives and change our societies in a rich pattern of interactions with culture and history. Here we will consider three principal demographic factors—life expectancy, fertility, and population—to reach some understanding of how the future will look and feel. This is a case in which the method used in most of this book doesn't work; since modern demography has not had enough time to reach a steady state it is quite possible that the demography of already-modern countries does not reveal how modern countries will behave in the future. Also, the future in this as in many other areas depends on future human choices and values, not on the inherent features of modernity.

The demographic symphony begins with the age-old pattern of life that existed until a few hundred years ago. Nature was hard and death was common. Those who survived disease, famine, and violence to die of old age lived nearly as long as those who die of old age today: on average about eighty-five years. (The average age at which people die of old age is called "life span," while the average age a newborn is expected to live is called "life expectancy.") Very few people, however, survived disease, famine, and violence long enough to die of old age; before and after the transition to agriculture, for tens of thousands of years, life expectancy remained about thirty years.

In the last two hundred years, Western Europe and North America, as well as Japan and some other countries, changed from traditional to modern societies. The population explosion of the last century, the remains of which are still being felt, came from the prevention of early death. Now, in the modern part of the world, life expectancy is near eighty and rising. The upper limit on life expectancy, unless we become able to and choose to manipulate genes to make fundamental changes in the nature of human beings, is not much more than eighty-five or ninety-five (the life span), so modern countries have already achieved close to ninety percent of the possible increase in life expectancy. Most of the rest of the world is only about fifteen years behind and gaining fast. Poor countries today have much higher life expectancy than the advanced countries did when they were at similar levels of income.

While death from old age does not appear in our medical statistics, approximately half the people in modern societies die of old age. Why do people die if they don't get sick or suffer violence? Because ten of the eleven of the body's internal systems needed to sustain life gradually become less effective beginning around age thirty. At first, the reduced effectiveness of our heart in moving blood, or our liver in removing toxic byproducts, doesn't hurt us because at age thirty our systems have much more capacity than they need for ordinary life—large reserves that are not needed, except perhaps in emergencies. But after age thirty these reserves begin gradually but steadily to decline, and after fifty years of reducing reserves, we reach a point where there are none left. Then something minor, such as an ordinary cold, happens and the body needs to call on the reserves. At some point, sufficient stress is placed on the reserves of one system or another, the system collapses, and we die of old age, though the attending doctor assigns some specific cause to put in the death report.

There are scientists who think we will soon be able to postpone death from old age. If good health in early years gives us more reserve capacity when the gradual decline from aging begins, death from old age would be postponed even if aging reduced our capacity at the same rate as before. Good health, and healthy lifestyles, may slow the rate at which aging reduces system capacity, and modern medicine and better protection from the elements may enable us to survive with slightly less reserves than we needed before. But since all of these effects have to work for *all* our essential systems, and none of them results in drastic changes, together they probably have the potential for adding relatively few more years to life span. The increases in life expectancy produced by modernization have already drastically changed the patterns of our lives, probably much more than they would be changed by adding ten or twenty years to life span.[1]

Modernization and demographic change go through characteristic patterns in time and space. Each country or region has its own modernization trajectory, which reflects the way new developments interact with local history. Trends move through the world as influences move from the more advanced to less advanced countries. The world pattern is the sum of the patterns of countries at different stages of more or less parallel development. The result is like a musical round with groups continually beginning a common tune at different times, except that the melodies are not exactly the same.

The basic drivers of demographic change are very simple: reductions in mortality at various ages, especially among infants, and reductions in the number of children borne by the average woman.

Before modernization, those women who lived to be thirty or forty had many children, but so many girls and women died young that the average girl baby had only about two children. Birth rates (the number of children born per thousand people) were high, but high death rates kept the population from rising. Under these circumstances, people often lived in large families, experienced much death, and rarely knew their grandparents or grandchildren. This demographic pattern also meant a society composed primarily of young people. Although people took on adult roles at sixteen or eighteen, or even younger, there were many more children needing schooling and care than there were old people in need of care. Practically nobody retired; people in their twenties were a much bigger share of the work force and citizenry than those in their fifties or sixties. Figure 6.1 shows the age pyramid for such a demographic pattern.

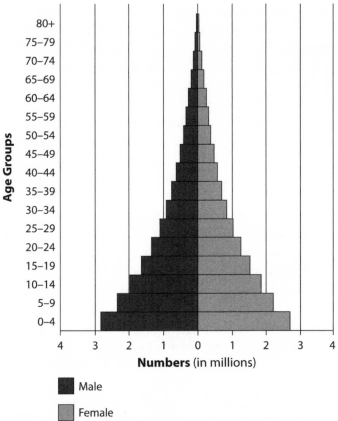

Figure 6.1. Population of Afghanistan, 2010

As modernization began to advance and spread though the world, death rates began to fall rapidly. The result was that fewer babies died; more girls became mothers, each with numerous children; and populations in the advanced countries, where death rates were falling, grew rapidly. These societies became older, but the shape of the age pyramid didn't change very much. Working people had many more children than old people to take care of.

The more advanced part of the world increased their population much more rapidly than less advanced parts, where death rates began to fall many years later.

Death rates were reduced primarily by food and soap, not doctors and hospitals. Having enough to eat, clean water to drink, sanitation, education, and public health measures—and later the defeat of infectious diseases, largely by vaccination and public health measures—were what drove death rates down. Today, medical miracles delivered by skilled doctors and advanced technology commonly extend the lives of many middle-aged and older people, and save many premature babies, but they provide a small share of the increase in overall life expectancy, even in advanced countries.

During this phase of demographic modernization, the continued high birth rates concealed an important change. Birth rates stayed high because there were more mothers in each generation. The population grew and stayed young, because death rates fell faster than birth rates. In every generation of this period of rapidly rising populations, however, the average mother had fewer children. In the United States, for example, fertility (the number of children borne by the average woman) began falling fairly steadily from about 6 two hundred years ago to 1.8 by 1970 (apart from the temporary rise during the famous baby boom from 1945 to 1960). This pattern became standard throughout Western Europe, where fertility mostly decreased throughout the twentieth century.

As this process goes on, four children come to seem to be a large family. People have fewer cousins and aunts and uncles, but grandparents become common. The adult world becomes dominated by people in their forties, fifties, and sixties, while those in their twenties and thirties generally are less important because they are learning and working their way up.

After World War II, in the second half of the twentieth century, a new demographic pattern began to shape life in the advanced countries. Lower fertility gradually raises the average age, and eventually the increase in the number of mothers is not enough to compensate for the fewer children of each mother. The result is gradually falling population and further aging.

At this stage, the typical mother has two children, and there are more children without siblings than there are families with three or more children. Most children will have only a few aunts and uncles and a few cousins, but more and more have great-grandparents. Old and very old people become a significant share of the population and more influential in politics and culture. No country has been at this stage long enough for the pattern to work through the whole age spectrum.

When the advanced countries first reach the stage of population decline, the less advanced countries are still at the early stage in which population is growing rapidly. So each group's share of total world population changes, in the opposite direction from the earlier changes when the advanced countries added population and the rest of the world had low growth. In part of the world, workers support many children and few aged; in other parts, workers support few children and many retirees. In some countries the average age is twenty or twenty-five, while in others it is forty or forty-five.

There is another important lagging pattern, although it is harder to measure. At first most people in demographically advanced societies with low death rates and small families have memories and strong cultural influences from the earlier stage of their society. Only after many years will we see a society that is completely formed by the experience of small families with few deaths except among the elderly, and of communities dominated by mature and elderly people.

So far, we have assumed that societies with low death rates will have fertility below replacement level, because that is what has happened almost universally. But we cannot say that below-replacement-level fertility is an inevitable result of modernization. Death rates are determined by the desire to live longer by using improving technology and increased wealth to postpone death. Fertility rates are independent of death rates; they depend on people's desire for children (as opposed to their desire for values that must be sacrificed for more children). If birth rates in a society are higher than death rates, then population will increase and a society will get younger.

Do we prefer a world with fifty million people or a world with fifty *billion* people? The world we get will depend on how many children people want to have and to raise. Everywhere in the world, with the partial exception of the United States, people are now choosing, or moving in the direction of choosing, to have so few children that unless they change their choices population will decline perhaps nearly one percent per year, which would mean cutting the world's population in half in less than a century.

Demographers have long proposed that after death rates stop falling, because of modern health and medicine, birth rates would eventually come into balance with death rates, and world population would level off. That is, for some time experts have been reassuring us that we are really in a "demographic transition." For millennia, they say, world population grew very slowly because high birth rates were matched by high death rates. (World population was only about 500 million in 1650, with an annual growth rate of 0.3 percent.) They explain that the recent "explosion" is only temporary, as falling birth rates catch up to falling death rates. During this period, they say, world population will increase by between seven and ten billion people.

In fact, the experts are importantly wrong. There is no justification for the comforting theory that in the long run, once we have adjusted to new living conditions and low death rates, birth and death rates will be more or less the same and world population will be reasonably stable. In modern conditions, death rates and birth rates have no real connection with each other. People deciding whether to have children don't pay any attention to death rates or to whether world population is rising or falling. We have no inherent protection against either indefinitely rising or falling population.

Originally, the idea that birth and death rates would eventually come into balance had the effect of assuring people that the "population explosion" would not last forever and therefore was not as frightening as they imagined. (Until a few years ago, Warren Buffett planned to give the bulk of his money to the effort to slow world population growth.) Now that fertility is falling nearly everywhere, and populations are getting ready to start declining, the idea of balanced birth and death rates protects people from having to think about world population declining for a long time, even indefinitely.

Despite the growing mass of data showing the disconnect between birth rates and death rates, the "official," most widely used long-term projections of world population, by the U.N. Population Division, still accept the idea that eventually birth rates will match death rates. As new data comes in showing that birth rates don't correlate to death rates, the Population Division just puts further into the future the date when birth rates will fall or rise to match death rates. In their report making projections to 2300 they say:

> Fertility is projected to stay below replacement level continuously for no more than 100 years per country over the period from 1950 forward, and to return to replacement after 100 years, or by the year 2175, whichever comes first.

The U.N. high projection is completely inconsistent with actual experience and can be ignored. The result is that the U.N. "medium" projection, which shows world population as still growing slightly in 2100, is not truly a medium estimate with the implication that it is the most likely case.

The other major institutional projection of future fertility, by the International Institute for Applied Systems Analysis (IIASA), is based on data rather than theories about fertility necessarily moving toward replacement level. The IIASA projections indicate that there is a high probability that world population will begin falling during this century.

In the long run—a number of centuries—world population size depends on human fertility. If women in the modern world have less than an average of about 2.1 children during their lifetime, as do the women in almost half the world now, then world population will steadily decline, quite possibly by a quarter or a half in a lifetime. If women in the modern world change the current fashion and decide to have more than an average of 2.1 children, then world population will steadily increase.

In other words, future population depends on the choices people make in the future about how many children they want to have. Almost anything can happen. There is no science that determines in which direction we will go. But the present pattern of behavior will lead to falling world population before the end of this century.

A reasonable guess, based on recent history, is that the average world fertility at the time that the whole world has just become modern will be something like 1.7 births per woman. Then, as far as we can know, fertility might rise over the course of fifty or a hundred years to a level of perhaps 2.5 births per woman, as new attitudes toward children and life predominate. Or it might not. It might stay at the original or a new level (or range) for one century or several before new ideas about family life again spread through the world, producing either a rise or a decline in average fertility. When the whole world is modern new ideas or values about family size might spread through the whole world almost simultaneously.

We have to ask whether modernity necessarily leads to below-replacement fertility as it leads to democracy. The fertility of every modern country has been below replacement level for at least twenty years. (While the United States fertility is about at replacement level, most of the modern countries are well below, ranging from 1.2 to 1.9.) Therefore the general approach of this book—that the history of now-modern countries reveals the future—would suggest that modernity implies below-replacement fertility. But, while it is plausible that modernity is inconsistent with fertility above 3, I don't believe that modernity is inconsistent with fertility above 2.1, that is, with a growing population. As there is relatively little difference in the size of families that produce below-replacement fertility of 1.9 and above-replacement fertility of 2.3, it is hard to see why one is compatible with modernity and not the other. Table 6.1 shows patterns of family size for fertility of 1.9 and two alternatives for 2.3.

An average one percent decline a year for the next five hundred years—as suggested by the behavior of half the world today—would reduce world population to about 250 million people, about what it was 1,000 years ago. An average one percent rise a year for five hundred years, on the other hand, would increase world population to perhaps 250 billion people, some forty times today's population. Both rates of change are feasible and plausible. Let's look at the history before considering these possibilities.

The fertility record since the last part of the twentieth century has been remarkably consistent throughout the world. In all of the 154 countries with populations over one million, fertility has been declining. So far, seventy countries have gone below replacement

Table 2   Alternative Family Patterns

A		B		C	
Fertility 1.9		Fertility 2.3		Fertility 2.3	
# of children	% of women	# of children	% of women	# of children	% of women
0	20%	0	10%	0	20%
1	18%	1	10%	1	10%
2	34%	2	40%	2	20%
3	18%	3	30%	3	35%
4+	10%	4+	10%	4+	15%

Case A is close to the current American pattern. Case B and C reach the larger total in different ways. In Case B, the number of women with 0 or 1 child is almost cut in half, and the most common family has 2 children. In Case C, there are still a large number of women with 0 or 1 child, but the most common family has 3 children. This could be a pattern in a society divided into family-friendly groups and groups with few children.

level. There are no countries in which it is clear that the fertility decline ended above replacement level, about 2.1 children per woman, although in a few countries the decline has been somewhat equivocal. In no country did fertility bounce back above 2.1 after hitting a bottom. The United States is the closest case to a bounce back to replacement level, and recently England and France have moved in that direction.

This pattern of virtually universal falling fertility to below replacement level in generally good conditions is unprecedented. We are seeing the first nearly worldwide decline in fertility to below replacement level—just as we are seeing the first fundamental change in mass living conditions. So we have no experience to shed light on what is likely to come next.

Eventually, and for the long term, fertility is what will determine population size. Sooner or later if each woman has fewer than 2.1 children, population will get older and start to become smaller. In all traditional societies, the youngest age group has been the largest, and each older age group was smaller. But when fertility stays below replacement level for a long time, the youngest age group is the smallest and each older group is larger, up to the group in which people begin dying from old age. The largest age group is people in their late fifties, and there are more people over sixty-five than under twenty. Future population pyramids will look something like Figure 6.2 for a while.

Never in history has there been a country with that kind of population. Unless there is a drastic change in human behavior, however, almost the whole world will be like that a little more than a century from now. Nobody can predict what it will feel like for a country to have such a population. Nor can anyone predict how people will feel about such an age pattern when it has been going on for so long that no one can remember what it was like for most women to have two, three, or more children and there were many young people in the society.

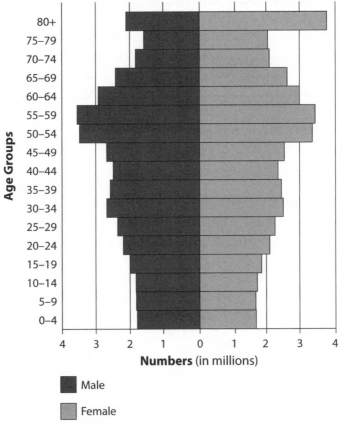

Figure 6.2. Population of Germany, 2020

A society in which many women, perhaps a quarter or a third, have no children, and few women have more than two children, feels very different from a society in which almost all women have two, three, or more children. In a world where fertility stays low, children will have few siblings, cousins, or aunts and uncles. We as a society have no experience with that kind of family life—except for some survivors of the Holocaust. Nor do we have any experience with societies in which children, and people caring for children, are such a small part of the scene and of most social arrangements.

For the long run, the question of the size of the world population depends primarily on whether people like small families and how they feel about the new kind of society in which children play a small role. In the kind of society that Western Europe, Japan, and many other parts of the world are developing now, children are rare and caring for children is a small part of people's lives. In the relatively recent societies that have shaped our consciousness, a typical woman would live with school-age children for some twenty-eight years of a seventy-year life (40 percent). In the new low-fertility societies, a typical woman will have school-age children for seventeen years of an eighty-five-year life (20 percent).

I see an early form of this difference moving back and forth between the United States and modern orthodox circles in Israel. In the United States there are a fair amount of children, but in social and business life parents are mostly expected to deal with the children without interfering with their other obligations. It is "unprofessional" to let family demands interfere with work arrangements more than occasionally. Three children make a big family, and people who have four or more children get strange looks, if not remarks.

In Israel, and especially the modern orthodox community, mores and arrangements are built to support families with children. Three children is the normal minimum, and four or five are common. A woman who has six children is more likely to be admired than regarded as weird or anti-social (though women with nine or ten children are part of a very different community). Both fathers and mothers normally leave work for child events, whether illnesses or class parties, without losing any professional status. Celebrations of births, bar mitzvahs, and weddings are a major share of social occasions.

In brief there is a clear—though modest—difference between the "feel" of Israeli and American societies as a cause and result of a difference in fertility of about one child per woman. Much of Western Europe now has fertility rates around 1.4 children per woman, almost one whole child less than the fertility required for modest growth rates.

When a pattern of small families and fewer children continues for a few generations, it is likely to be built into expectations and behavior of all kinds and quite possibly to make the social world quite unwelcoming to families with three of more children. On the other hand, if this pattern continues, many people may begin to feel that there is something missing, that they have lost out by not making children and family a bigger part of their lives. Society might become divided into two parts, one that is child oriented, populated mostly by couples with three, four, or more children who socialize mostly with other similar families, and perhaps with women who have children without marriage. The other part of society—in which many women don't marry, don't have children, or have at most one child—may feel different from the family-oriented group and may develop different behaviors and attitudes.

Children in the family-oriented society are likely to feel most comfortable marrying people who grew up in the family-friendly part of society. So a country might have two distinguishable components, one with a fertility not much above one and the other with a fertility of about three. Wherever this happens, the part of society with low fertility would tend to decline quite rapidly while the family-oriented part of society would get larger. If the fertility patterns were to continue for some generations, total or average fertility would rise almost to the level of the higher group. Of course, this tendency could be speeded or slowed by individuals who decide to cross over from one group to the other.

Just as each country may tend to divide itself into communities with different attitudes about children, so can different countries take different paths. If it were not for recent history, one might have expected that Italy would be a family-oriented country with high fertility, while Sweden would be dominated by the "modern" pattern of few children. So far, however, they have behaved alike: Italy and Sweden currently have nearly the same levels of fertility, about 1.3 children per woman. In the future, as all countries are wealthy, with similar economies, national cultures and traditions may lead the people of some countries to value children more highly, and thus have more children, than those of other countries.

The one inherent element of demography that favors rising rather than falling population is the fact that when the world (or any part of it) is divided into two populations, one with rising population and one with falling population, then the part with falling population eventually drops out of the picture. Imagine a world in which 10 percent of the people are child lovers with a fertility of 2.5, and the other 90 percent have a fertility of 1.7, either because they don't like children or because they want to give their children every advantage and lots of attention. To predict the long-run population of that world, you could ignore the low-fertility group, because it would die out. The long-run population of the world would be the population of the child-lovers, which would double every seventy years or so, and in a few centuries would exceed the original total world population, even though very few of the originally dominant low fertility group would remain.

Of course, this artificial example assumes that the average fertility of each group stayed the same and people didn't move from one group to the other. Things don't work that way. But the principle that future population is more influenced by the high-fertility component of population, if that high fertility is stable, is an important principle that will to some degree shape the future of world population. But it must be applied carefully. Today the world can be divided into high- and low-fertility countries, but in almost all the high-fertility countries fertility is falling fairly rapidly or very rapidly. We can't tell whether they will continue to be high-fertility countries after they complete the stage, which all countries go through, of falling fertility.

While it is true that fertility in modern countries now is below replacement levels, low fertility is not only a result of modernity. Some non-modern countries, such as Iran and Bangladesh, have rapidly declining fertility, and China's rate has been below replacement level for a generation. In the future, some modern societies may well put a high value on children, have fertility above 2.1, and grow. Others, of course, like the typical pattern today, will value other things more than children and therefore have fewer children and eventually a declining population.

Shifting attitudes about raising children is a good example of the many open, changeable, and unpredictable features of modern life. All the essential defining features of modern life—long lives, education, comfortable conditions, commercial international economies, change, choice, and so on—are compatible with fertility rates above or below replacement. There is no way of knowing in which parts of the modern world, or in which future centuries, there will be low fertility. Now, below-replacement fertility is an idea that is sweeping the whole world. Maybe it will continue to be true that just about the whole world has essentially a single attitude toward the value of children, with modest differences from place to place. But it is also possible that different countries (or non-national populations) will have significantly different values and behavior.

In short, one of the things we don't know about the modern world of the future is how many people will live in it. Six hundred years from now—as far in the future as Columbus was in the past—the world could be home to anywhere between a hundred million and a hundred billion people, all wealthy, free, and peaceful.

Some readers may believe that the world is not big enough for a hundred billion people. While I do not agree, there is no need to consider the question here. Unless human behavior changes drastically from the current pattern (low or falling fertility), world population will fall for at least a century, beginning about the middle of this century. If after that it turns around and rises for a few centuries, people will have to begin to think about the earth's capacity. By then there will be a lot more technology and knowledge, and the question is likely to look rather different from how it looks today.

In brief: not our problem.

NOTE

1. But the "optimistic" scientists have something more dramatic in mind—finding and manipulating the genes responsible for aging to slow the process, so that our systems don't lose capacity so fast. Scientists can debate whether this will become possible, and ethicists are already debating whether it would be a boon for humankind.

Dr. Leon Kass, Chairman of the President Bush's Commission on Bioethics, for example, has written about the undesirability of changing life span because of the effect that longer life span would have on the character of life. It seems clear that immortality—in the Woody Allen sense of living forever—would clearly require changing almost everything in the understanding of what it means to be human—something not to be done lightly. But what about increasing life span from eighty-five to ninety-five years? Or to 150 or 200 years, which some claim will be possible?

7

THE FUTURE OF WORK

What might life be like if we as a median family earned $1 million a year in today's dollars (twenty times as much as the current median of $50,000)?

We would have a bigger house that is better decorated and equipped. We might want to eat gourmet meals every night, so some of us might look into having a chef. But if a chef also earned the median income, we couldn't afford to keep her full-time without spending our whole income on her. Undoubtedly, there would be some very advanced ways of organizing to enable a chef to produce gourmet meals for many people. Restaurants, caterers, and food suppliers would be using new technology to come as close as possible to providing people with dinner at home, almost like having a chef in the kitchen. It is also possible that many people would prefer being chefs to doing other work, and would be satisfied with much less than the median income. If that were true, people with the median income could afford to have a chef to cook at least some of their meals. Or someone in the family would become a chef and reduce or eliminate the amount of time working for money.

We would want to have vacations. But land, and therefore hotels, in central Paris or near the beach in Cancun would be very expensive. In fact beaches all over the world would be developed with ambiances to match every taste, at a high price. Improved travel technology would enable us to go to beaches wherever they are,[1] though the fare would have to include the cost of a very expensive pilot (unless piloting were so popular that it had become a low-wage job, or we could fly ourselves). A good share of our money would go to pay for expensive services: trainers and coaches of all kinds, tutors, tour guides, art advisors. A good share of community and private resources would probably go to maintaining a high standard of environmental quality.

As technology advances, all physical products become less expensive. Fewer people work to produce such physical goods as electricity or such physical services as communications and transportation. More and more people try to do jobs that machines cannot do. That means they have to spend more time learning special skills or developing service talents, while other people figure out how machines can do more of the work that a short time ago people were required to do.

If we want to learn the effect on people's lives of becoming ten times richer, we should look at the effect on our lives of our being ten times richer than people were in the United States around the turn of the last century. Some of the changes won't happen again. A good part of the population then did not have enough clean food or drinking water, and lived in crowded, dirty, and unhealthy houses. As a result, on average, they were smaller and sicker, and they died younger. The income we have now has almost eliminated such conditions. Most of the poor in the United States today are healthier, apart from self-damaging behavior, than most rich people were a century ago—partly because of new medical science and partly because of better living conditions. We can't expect such an improvement from the next tenfold increase in wealth, though we can't know what other improvements might come from new science.

Another change that has come with our increase in wealth is that we can do things we couldn't do before, such as visit our children for the weekend even if they live hundreds of miles away, or talk to them every night on the phone. Certainly people a century from now will be able to do things we cannot do now. Part of our higher income will be used to pay for those things.

On the other hand, a hundred years ago many middle income people had servants in the house to wash dishes and make beds. In our richer world, only very few people can afford to have a servant to wash the dishes. (Perhaps when incomes are much higher, and service is even more expensive, people may avoid dishwashing by using recyclable disposable dishes that are as attractive as good chinaware is today.) In former times, there were people around to help you everywhere, in stores, on trains, in hotels. In rich countries, most of these helpers are gone, replaced by technology-aided self-service.

In a world in which few people had much money, it did not cost too much to put yourself in an exclusive place, where you were separated from ordinary people, or doing things that ordinary people didn't do. Now it takes much more money to get away from crowds and ordinary people. As wealth multiplies again, we should expect this trend to continue.

There's no reason the same pattern cannot apply to the next ten-fold increase in income: unimaginable changes in technology; some technology used to substitute for human labor, some technology used to do things previously impossible; human time becoming more valuable and therefore most people doing increasingly sophisticated, demanding, and often personal work; and higher living standards combined with increasingly demanding tastes, spread more and more throughout the population (no longer simply the privilege of elites).

While people grew richer, and used more material, they used less and less material per dollar that they spent. So the demand for energy and raw materials grew more slowly than total wealth or expenditures. This trend will almost certainly continue, and it is seen all over the world. Partly for this reason, the increase in wealth will not be stopped by a shortage of raw materials or of places to safely put the garbage.

Since the amount a society produces is simply the number of hours worked multiplied by the productivity of the average hour of work, the process of steadily increasing wealth can only stop through some combination of slowing productivity growth or less work. How might these happen?

First, we have to recognize that productivity doesn't depend only on the worker and his or her enterprise; it also depends on how the country is running, on what choices the society has made in striking a balance between high productivity and other conflicting goals. Societies inevitably pursue many goods—equality, environmental quality, consumer protection, investment transparency, and so on—that inherently conflict, at least slightly, with efforts to increase productivity, but almost all goals can be pursued to self-defeating extremes at which sacrifices are far in excess of benefits. Even when they are pursued wisely, many goals and values are in conflict with the goal of increasing productivity.

No overall decision is made by Congress, the president, or voters about whether to prefer economic efficiency or other social goals. The question is fought out on a thousand separate fronts. The overall balance achieved by all of these separate political conflicts determines how supportive a country's environment is for people's struggles to increase productivity. Productivity can only continue growing if the business environment is not too harmful.

As a country gets richer and richer, for example, the political environment tilts further in favor of other social goals and against what is needed to maintain productivity growth. The more people feel that a country is rich enough, the more they will favor actions that have the side effect of preventing the country from getting richer. The result is likely to be that median family income will never reach a million dollars or even half a million.

This conflict between economic efficiency and other goals is waged separately in each country. While there will be international influences on these struggles, to an important extent each country will decide how to strike its own balance. The result is that countries that remain concerned about getting richer will have higher incomes than countries that prefer other values. Also, countries that are smarter about pursuing other goals in ways that don't reduce efficiency will have more productivity growth.

In the very long run, it may well turn out that the richest countries are those that care most about being rich. Other countries, even if they are more talented or hardworking, would be less rich if they limited productivity by social choices that preferred other values that conflict with productivity.

We can thus limit or stop growth by spending time and resources in less-productive ways (though a society may find such "non-productive" goals extremely valuable and worth the sacrifice). The other way to limit or stop growth is to do less work. As people get richer, and earn more from an hour's work, they may decide to work fewer hours. Perhaps when the median family can earn a half a million dollars if it works as much as a median family does today (3,000 hours a year divided among three family members), that family may find they can buy everything they want—including protection against old age, illness, and hard times—with only a quarter of a million dollars per year, so they may decide to work only 1,500 hours a year. If many families make such decisions, the country will produce less and there will be less income for all families together.

If productivity keeps growing, however, average income will also grow unless people reduce even further the amount they work. Fifty years after median family income is held at a quarter of a million dollars a year by the decision to work only 1,500 hours a year, that income could double, unless the family decided to cut the their working time down to 750 hours a year.

There is another way that productivity could stop growing, or even begin to fall. People could decide to work at what they like to do rather than at what they are most efficient at doing. Someone who could earn one million dollars a year as a lawyer might decide to make pottery or poetry instead, earning much less. Others may decide to have a winery, or a ranch, even though the earnings are low, because they like the lifestyle. Statistically, they will have low productivity, even though they value very highly the psychological rewards of their work.

John Maynard Keynes wrote about these kinds of possibilities as long ago as 1930:

> The economic problem is not—if we look into the future—the permanent problem of the human race . . . I see us free, therefore, to return to some of the most sure and certain principles of religion and

traditional virtue—that avarice is a vice, that the exaction of usury is a misdemeanor, and the love of money is detestable, that those who walk most truly in the paths of virtue and sane wisdom who take least thought for the morrow. We shall once more value ends above means and prefer the good to the useful. We shall honor those who can teach us how to pluck the hour and the day virtuously and well. The delightful people who are capable of taking direct enjoyment of things, the lilies of the field who toil not, neither do they spin. But beware! The time for all this is not yet. For at least another hundred years we must pretend to ourselves and to everyone that fair is foul and foul is fair; for foul is useful and fair is not. Avarice, and usury, and precaution must be our gods for a little longer still. For only they can lead us out of the tunnel of economic necessity into the daylight.[2]

Most simply, per capita income will stop rising when enough people, as individuals and as communities, value benefits that cannot be bought with money more than they value money and what it can buy. Although there is little statistical evidence that people with incomes ten times higher than the average are less concerned about earning money than are those with lower incomes (that is, as people get richer, they do not tend to work less), that may change in the future. Perhaps when the whole population multiplies income tenfold, people will be less motivated to work for money. Despite the absence of evidence, it is possible that at some significantly higher level of income, people's motivation to increase their income will be less than it is now.

When a large share of people's work is not determined by efforts to earn as much money as possible, and when a large share of the benefits that people seek are not purchased with money, conventional accounting and economics becomes a much less effective way of understanding behavior.

Consider the example of an engineer who can earn, say, $200,000 a year working for an engineering firm, but who decides to spend his time on what had been his hobby, running a kennel to breed and sell Great Dane puppies, where he could only earn $50,000. Conventional accounting would say that he and the country have become less productive. Instead of the $200,000 dollars worth of engineering work he had produced before, he now produces only $50,000 worth of Great Dane puppies, using the same number of hours of work. But this doesn't tell the whole story. He also produces some satisfaction for himself, satisfaction that he can't sell and therefore doesn't enter the national accounts. But it is satisfaction for which he is willing to sacrifice $150,000 minus his tax savings. Shouldn't the national accounts take credit for producing this satisfaction, if there were some objective way of measuring it?

Another way of looking at the same example is to say that the bookkeeping for the kennel was wrong. It showed that the engineer was paid a $50,000 salary (or made a $50,000 profit, if he didn't take a salary), but it didn't include in its costs the engineer's sacrifice of the money he could have earned by engineering. If opportunity cost were used, the kennel should have charged itself $200,000 for the engineer's time, producing a net loss. But this loss would be made up by charging the engineer the $150,000 he was willing to pay for the satisfaction he got from running the kennel. So the kennel would have broken even, paying the engineer $200,000 and producing $50,000 worth of Great Dane puppies and $150,000 of the engineer's satisfaction. This would make the country look richer, and would increase the taxes paid to the government, but it would only work if the engineer had $150,000 a year to buy his satisfaction. Such an accounting implies that each person is some kind of slave who has an obligation to do whatever work is most productive, and that each person should pay for any satisfaction he or she gets even if that satisfaction has no cost except for opportunity cost. Obviously we can't get into such an Alice-in-Wonderland system of accounting.

Here's what happens with this example, which stands for all kinds of mixed-motivation activity that can be called work or play, under conventional accounting. If the engineer uses his time to raise the puppies and gives them away, he is not working; the country has fewer hours of work that year, with no reduction of productivity, just smaller output because of fewer hours. If the engineer sells the puppies, he counts as working. But since he earns (and produces)

$50,000 instead of $200,000, the country's productivity is reduced. Either way, the country's output is reduced (because the satisfaction isn't counted), because fewer hours were worked or because the same number of hours were worked but average productivity was lowered.

What "really" happens with these kinds of behavior is that productivity and wealth continue to grow, but some of the wealth comes in the form of "non-economic satisfaction" and is not counted.

There are two implications from this example. Welfare or satisfaction can continue to increase after economic growth stops. We should understand that conventional accounting is a very incomplete report of what is happening in an economy or a society. Even today, much of what is important is not recorded, or recorded inappropriately, and this mismatch of data and reality will get worse if increased wealth more and more leads people to be concerned with considerations other than money.

The mismatch between economic measures and a more complete understanding of reality works in both directions, both overstating and understating real benefits and overstating and understating real costs. Most of the work and discussion on these issues has been devoted to showing how conventional accounting ignores human and social costs, such as harm to the environment. But there is no reason not to assume that conventional accounting also ignores benefits—decisions made by people to support values that improve their lives.

Trying to adjust economics to include non-financial benefits and costs would be an immense, perhaps hopeless task. Consider a teacher earning a modest salary. He might be earning the most he can or only a fraction of his potential. The teacher's motivation for taking the job could be any combination of reasons: because he found it pleasant or satisfying; because the hours and arrangements were convenient; because it was the best combination of salary, benefits, and job security he could find; or because of a desire to do something good for the community. The teacher might not be very clear in his mind about the balance of motivations, and the balance might change over time. From a social policy perspective, however, the mix of motivations matters a good deal if you are asking how to get better teachers, or how to get teachers to do a better job.

Of course, societies will not be uniform. Today, work is important for at least one person in almost all families. Income is a major concern for most people when they choose their work, though it is already true that many people sacrifice potential income (productivity) to get other rewards from their work (or to avoid work they don't like). If average income rises by three or ten times, it seems likely that work and income will become less important to people. Some will respond by not working at all, or by working fewer hours a year, or fewer years. Others will work at doing things they like—and might even even pay to do—such as arts or crafts, or public service. Others will continue to work for money because that is the kind of work they like. Some people have a taste for efficiency and effectiveness, or command and responsibility, rather than for beauty or harmony.

One result is that the concept of work will have to become much more subtle and complicated. Today, we usually get away with assuming that work is that which is done for money, or to produce something the worker wants. As earned income becomes a much smaller part of people's decisions about work and about what to do with their time, however, we will have to develop new concepts of the meaning of work.

If greatly increased wealth sharply reduces people's motivation to work for money, they could respond in quite different ways. Table 3 illustrates three different responses (the numbers used in the table are rough estimates, sometimes even guesses).

In all three cases—A, B, and C—the motivation to work for money has been so greatly reduced that instead of devoting 55 percent of "worktime" to maximizing income, which is a reasonable estimate for today, only 25 percent of worktime is devoted to maximizing income.

In Alternative A, people keep on working almost as many hours as now, but most of the work becomes "avocational" work, that is, work chosen because it is either pleasant or done for the benefit of the community or both, and because it produces inncome (though

Table 3 How People's 2,000 Hours per Year of "Work Time" Is Used Now and Three Ways It Might Be Used When Productivity Is Much Greater*

	Percentage of "Work Time"			
	Now	Alt. A	Alt. B	Alt. C
Work				
employed for money in highest productivity jobs (including self-employed)	55%	25%	25%	25%
employed for money in avocational jobs public service work art or craft with earning potential lifestyle jobs (lifeguard, wilderness guide)	14%	40%	15%	15%
home-making and child-care	3%	4%	6%	5%
working to produce for self home repair and improvement gardening investment activities and other	4%	6%	8%	5%
	76%	76%	54%	50%
"Work-like" activities				
serious efforts to do something hard, with standards e.g., art, craft, sport	2%	3%	12%	4%
formal or systematic education	9%	10%	18%	12%
	11%	13%	30%	16%
Non-work				
active sports, games, hiking, etc.	2%	2%	3%	8%
learning, reading, spiritual activities	2%	2%	3%	8%
"hanging out," partying, enjoying the moment	5%	5%	4%	10%
watching television and other passive entertainment	3%	3%	5%	8%
	12%	12%	15%	34%

*Numbers are estimated or speculative. Normal chores come out of non-working time, as do sleep, normal amusements, meals, and so forth.

less income than high-productivity jobs). Avocational work includes a wide range of things, some of which may earn nearly as much as work for income, such as teaching school or managing welfare organizations, and some of which earn barely enough to be counted as work, such as most poetry writing and craft work.

In alternative B, the decline in hours of work to maximize income is made up for mainly by increases in other work and in "work-like activity"—that is, serious, demanding effort with an inherent discipline. There is only an increase by three percent in the time spent on play.

Alternative C is a big move toward Keynes's lilies of the field who take pleasure in the moment, attentive to ends and not to means. But even in this scenario only a third of people's work time is used for play, that is, for being like the lilies of the field. Probably more "playful" scenarios are also possible.

All three alternatives would involve a massive change in price structure in the economy. The supply of labor for all kinds of jobs would be drastically changed. There would be fewer people competing for unattractive jobs; if the need for such work is unchanged, salaries for those jobs would increase. On the other hand, there would be many more people competing for attractive or idealistic work, and presumably wages for those jobs would decline. These changes in cost would produce changes in price, which would change the amount people would buy of the products or services that become much more or less expensive. The changes in workers' motivation would also change the way work is done. Companies would organize work much more to increase its attractiveness than to increase the output per hour. They would still be pursuing efficiency, because if an employer can get workers for half the pay by making the job more attractive, and workers are not looking mostly for money, the employer can profit from increasing other costs and reducing pay.

The GNP per capita for each of the three alternatives could be the same as it is now, because we are assuming that the changed pattern of work is the result of increased productivity and income. Therefore, as much output can be produced with many fewer hours of work. In Alternative A, productivity is greatly reduced (because avocational work still counts as work but is less productive). In Alternatives B and C, both hours of work and productivity are reduced.

What we are interested in is the effect on society of these different patterns of work. How different is a society when many fewer people are working primarily for income? How different is a society when people work many fewer hours? And does it matter if the people who are not working are doing something "work-like" or if they are just playing?

In the modern era (toward which the whole world is moving now), work for income is as much at the center of human life as it has always been—one of the important ways in which the modern era is like the past. Work for the purpose of production is perhaps the principal activity of most people. The era that follows the modern era may well be different, in that work for production may no longer be so central to human life. Most characteristics of the modern era would carry over to a society of play. That is, people would live long, comfortable, safe lives in freedom, with plenty of choice, in urban settings with a commercial worldwide economy and advancing science and technology. But life in which society is shaped by pleasure-seeking, or idleness, would be very different from the modern life we can see. Or maybe it depends on how people seek pleasure. Aldous Huxley and others have speculated about the effect of people getting pleasure from drugs. Other forms of undisciplined and unconstrained pleasure-seeking, of life devoted to play, would also make a very different world from the modern world. It might be almost as hard for people in that world to understand our lives as it is for us to understand the lives of people working the land and living ignorantly in villages.

Any of these different worlds could begin to appear within a few centuries after the world becomes modern. However, they all depend on rich societies not doing things that sharply reduce the growth of productivity. Without productivity growth, incomes won't rise and people will not move away from work. If you are afraid of the harmful effects of increasing wealth, then you should favor taxes and regulations that prevent productivity from increasing, because presumably if productivity doesn't increase people will keep working.

Or, to put it another way, perhaps the coming modern era will only continue if societies do things that prevent the continued increase in productivity. If not, sustained growth of productivity will end the modern era as it ended the traditional era.

GNP per capita in traditional worlds was mostly in the range of $400 per year (in 1990 dollars), with advanced civilizations, such as the Roman, reaching $800 and Western Europe, just before sustained growth began, perhaps a little more than $1,700. Countries become modern when they have per capita incomes around $20,000 (in 1990 dollars). So we can say that multiplying per capita income by twenty to thirty times was enough to change the traditional world to the modern world.

It would not be surprising if another multiplication of GNP per capita by twenty or thirty times, if it happens, would bring as big a change in the character of human life as the change from Rome to today. On the other hand, most of the fourteen characteristics of the modern world (see table 1) that we have discussed would not be decisively changed by such a multiplication of per capita income. People would still live long, healthy lives, among their children and grandchildren (if they so choose), and they will have similar political and religious freedoms. In any event, this book is about the history of the future, not the future of the future, so I don't have to take a position on what happens *after* modernity. But it does seem possible that multiplication of income by forty times would completely change the role of work in human life and bring us to a new, postmodern era.

NOTES

1. This is why the popular statement they "they aren't creating beachfront—or lakefront—property anymore" is essentially wrong. *Accessible* beachfront property is still being created, and will be for a long time.

2. John Maynard Keynes, *Essays in Persuasion* (Norton, 1963), p. 366ff.

EPILOGUE

The Desperate
Problems of the Future

This sketch of the history of the future suggests that by the end of the next century, the world will consist largely of modern countries. While there may be a hangover from the traditional world in sub–Saharan Africa, that region will generally be understood as a special case, a major but temporary problem for the world. Two hundred years from now, modernity—as I have defined it, based on the characteristics of the twenty-odd countries that are modern today—will be the mainstream of the world, if it doesn't cover the entire world.

As the world becomes modern, people will face a new set of problems, and it is not too soon to begin thinking about how to deal with them. These new problems pose significant threats to our character, our nature as human beings, and how we feel about our lives, that is, our sense of purpose, our happiness, and our goodness. Before we turn to the new problems, however, let's review the reasons for believing that we will no longer be dealing with the old problems that have shaped humankind from our beginning.

Traditionally, the main problem that dominated human lives was lack of wealth. Most people's time and effort was spent obtaining resources to have enough to eat and to meet other physical needs and desires, at what now looks like a very low level. At the beginning of the modern era, people will still need to devote a good portion of their time to earning a living, except for people who are content to have much less than the average, but generally people will not have to fear poverty and societies will have ample resources (although they may feel poor). Of course, those who get their satisfaction from having more than other people will still face the endless challenge of keeping materially ahead (although in a world in which many people are likely to be satisfied to coast, it will be easier for the competitive to get ahead).

Is it realistic to expect that by the end of next century, all the world, with the possible exception sub–Saharan Africa, will be at least as wealthy as France and Japan are today? How could Bangladesh, with its teeming millions of people mostly living in shacks a few feet above sea level, become a modern country like Canada or Italy so soon?

The short answer is that two hundred years ago France, Canada, Japan, and all the modern countries were as poor as Bangladesh is today. Furthermore, it is now much easier to increase productivity and wealth than it ever has been, because of all the wealth in the world and because of widespread experience with the process of growing wealthy. Moreover, it is in the interest of the richer countries for the poor countries to become rich: while we like having cheap labor in other countries, we like having rich customers there even more, and we gain by having more advanced competition for our suppliers.

Bangladesh, or Myanmar, will have to change in many ways to become a modern country. But two centuries is a long time. If we recall how much we have changed since Andrew Jackson's time, we can appreciate the likelihood that countries now so far behind economically might become modern before the end of the next century. Anyhow, there is no deadline. The basic picture is still the same if it takes them fifty or a hundred years more than I estimate.

The fundamental point is that we should not be surprised that countries change from traditional to modern, just as people change from children to adults. We should not expect countries to stay as they are, however far behind they are now. Poverty has become a passing phase; it is no longer the eternal condition of human beings. In looking at the pattern of differences among countries today, we should understand it not as a representation of the inevitable nature of the world but as a snapshot taken at one instant in time of countries that are changing on different schedules.

Another major problem that has bedeviled humankind is tyranny. Although fewer than half the countries in the world today are free countries, in which people govern themselves and have protected political rights, people in the modern world will not have to engage in struggles to escape from tyranny. Given all the tyranny we see today, with its long history and deep roots in human nature, this expectation may seem to be mere wishful thinking, a projection of idealistic values onto a cruel world that offers too desolate a landscape for them to take root.

The brief answer to this pessimism of the present is a simple syllogism. Because of the nature of modern economies, modern countries cannot be tyrannies. A world in which most countries are modern and the rest remain stuck for many generations at less-advanced stages is not plausible. Therefore, sooner or later all countries will move toward democratic forms of government, if only to release latent productive forces, and then become modern.

Pessimistic doubts are often right in the short term, but they are much less reasonable for a time as long as two centuries. Sooner or later the syllogism above will work. I can concede the strength of the forces preserving tyranny, and accept that they may well succeed for a long time, but eventually the world's problem will no longer be tyranny. And "eventually" doesn't mean five hundred or a thousand years.

The third problem the world will have to do without, once it becomes modern, is the war system. The war system has been the traditional international reality; the freedom, safety, and influence of countries has largely depended on their military strength and alliances. This made military power, and the diplomatic flux of alliance-building, the center of national policy, and from time to time led to war. But the war system cannot survive if there are only modern countries whose wealth, power, and influence is based on the creative work of free peoples, and whose societies are founded on law, politics, and negotiation, with no national role for violence.

Just as innate human aggression has had to adapt to the disappearance of, say, dueling, it will have to adapt to the disappearance of the war system and the role of war in human life. Struggles for power, and the exercise of soaring personal and national ambition, will be expressed in other ways than through the use or threat of military force.

The real-world evidence supporting this analytic argument is the current behavior of Western Europe, where influence does not depend on military strength and no country feels threatened militarily by any other country in that formerly war-prone part of the world. It is now a region, unlike any in history, where countries' security mostly depends on the character of neighboring countries, not on military strength or alliances.

This prediction, perhaps more than any other, may seem naive, a denial of millennia of human experience and human character. True, it *is* a denial of human history, a denial that is required because modern countries are so profoundly different from the countries that enacted human history in the past. The whole point is to recognize how different modern countries are from all societies that went before. When we put our minds to recognizing the differences between life and experience in modern countries and that of traditional countries, and when we consider the different incentives modern countries have in making their foreign policy compared to the incentives and fears of traditional countries, we will not be surprised that there will be profound differences between the history of the past and the history of the future.

Much scorn was heaped on Francis Fukuyama by people who thought he was arguing that the "end of history" had already come. Of course, his claim was not that history had ended, but "only" that the end of the history of the evolution of forms of government was coming and could already be seen. In order to avoid similar undeserved scorn, I should emphasize and reemphasize that the world is not modern now, and will not be modern for at least a century. Much of what I talk about as part of the past is still active in the world today, and will continue to be active for the rest of our lives and those of our grandchildren. Today we are still living in a transition period—long for us, short for history—in which examples of the modern coexist with much that will eventually come to be seen as part of the past.

If the modern world will be wealthy, free, and peaceful, what have we got to worry about? Plenty. If there is no higher value than comfortable self-preservation and self-satisfaction, too much wealth and freedom may bring misery, cruelty, waste, and dissolution. In *Democracy in America*, Tocqueville envisioned "an innumerable multitude of men, all equal and alike, incessantly endeavoring to procure the petty and paltry pleasures with which they glut their lives."

Many people, usually those who do the most for society, need challenges. In the old days, their strength was forged in struggles to overcome poverty, defeat a tyrant, or win a war. Those challenges will hardly exist when the world as a whole is modern. Life will seem too easy. There will be no dragons to slay, or at least the traditional ones will be gone.

When my children were young and complained, I would say that I didn't want to deprive them of adversity. While this was partly a joke, we see many examples of children who are spoiled by being too protected from adversity. In the future, we may have to worry about whole societies that are protected from most of the traditional sources of adversity. People used to say "the devil finds work for idle hands," and he likely also finds work for idle souls. We did not evolve for easy lives; a big adjustment will be required when most people have it easy.

Prosperity does not dissolve all social problems; in fact, it often creates new ones. Increased income in a society that cares only about material acquisition may lead to hedonism and ennui, or corrode community. It may be culturally and socially pernicious. Fred Hirsch, in his *Social Limits of Growth* and E.J. Mishan, in *The Costs of Economic Growth*, argue that certain kinds of economic development threaten a society's social and moral fabric. Irving Kristol warned that as societies become wealthier, they "seem to breed all sorts of new social pathologies and discontents . . . Crime and other forms of delinquency increase with increasing prosperity. Alcoholism and drug addiction also rise . . . The emphasis is placed on the pleasures of consumption rather than the virtues of work." Octavio Paz addresses the same concerns in his Nobel Lecture (December 8, 1990):

> For the first time in history mankind lives in a sort of spiritual wilderness and not, as before, in the shadow of those religious and political systems that consoled us at the same time as they oppressed us . . . It is a dangerous experience. It is also impossible to know whether the tensions and conflicts unleashed in this privatization of ideas, practices and beliefs that belonged traditionally to the public domain will not end up by destroying the social fabric.

According to Nietzsche and Fukuyama, modern civilization weakens our character by eliminating life or death challenges and the need for bravery. Heroism may be the highest and most noble state of human life. Although few people can actually be heroes, tales of heroism, and the potential need for it, have been important influences on human civilization. What will happen to people living in a world in which there is almost no need for, or room for, heroism?

People need to feel purpose in their lives. Many people are strengthened by believing that they have some reason for living beyond just getting along and caring for their families. In traditional societies, many people are shaped by the higher purpose of fighting poverty or tyranny. Without these struggles, what will inspire people with a sense that they serve a higher end in life?

We will have to learn to deal with self-destructive temptations that may inhere in democratic forms of government, or at least in some forms of democracy. Also, the logic of individualism and rejection of authority—which played a powerful role in shaping the modern—may lead to destructive extremes.

Certainly the modern world will not be paradise. People will have an ample supply of personal troubles. There will be murders, and child abuse, and perhaps terrorism, along with all kinds of less-dramatic personal agonies caused by bad luck or human weaknesses. So anyone looking for people in need of help will be able to find ample opportunities to spend time and effort helping others. But the big dramatic struggles against poverty, tyranny, and war will be largely gone.

The vision of this book is not messianic or blithely utopian. It remains agnostic about whether life will be better or people happier in the modern world. Contrary to the socialists (Trotsky once said that in the socialist future "man would become immeasurably stronger, wiser, freer, his body more harmoniously proportioned, his movement more rhythmic, his voice more musical"), I assume that human nature will *not* change—if it does, that change could be for the worse or for the better. Out of the crooked timber of humanity, Kant remarked, no straight thing was ever made. Many problems will remain insoluble. Crisis, anxiety, and the human capacity for brutality will not disappear. Stupidity, sin, and meanness will not vanish. Only some social ills can be eradicated, and others will arise. There will be dangers from decadence and utopianism. The progress that this book brings into high relief does not require or guarantee *moral* progress. That is the task for the future, when people will have greater freedom of choice than at any time in human history.

As John Maynard Keynes put it in his essay "Economic Possibilities for Our Grandchildren" (in *Essays in Persuasion*):

> The economic problem, the struggle for subsistence, always has been hitherto the primary, most pressing problem of the human race. If the economic problem is solved, mankind will be deprived of its traditional purpose . . . For the first time since his creation man will be faced with his real, his permanent problem—how to use his freedom from pressing economic cares, how to occupy his leisure, which science and compound interest will have won for him, to live wisely and agreeably and well.

In the end, affluence, freedom, and peace will only introduce a new set of questions. In fact, removing the challenges and adversity that have always shaped human character may very well leave us needing new tools to overcome human weakness.

Another problem that may haunt the future is the danger to family. Marriage, that is, long-term relationships between men and women who together raise children, has been one of the fundamental structures of civilized life. Traditionally, long-lasting partnerships between men and women were based on men's greater strength and ability to deal with violent threats, and on the need for the greater efficiency of two people working together as a single economic unit. These and other underlying benefits of monogamy were reinforced by a variety of social constructs and by law, religion, and community pressures, not to mention the role of romance, which is also undercut by modern ways.[1]

It is clear that generally both men and women gain from being part of a relationship based on long-term commitment, and that on average children do better when raised by a pair of parents. But these benefits require sacrifices and discipline, and as people face increasing temptations to do without marriage or to give it up, a large reduction in human welfare may result.

Marriage is now losing, or has already lost, most of the supports it had until recently. As violence becomes less common, women have less need for a physical protector. As it becomes easier to earn enough to live on, the efficiency benefit of marriage becomes less important. Neither law nor community standards now hold couples together. Current sexual standards reduce marriage's advantage as a source of sexual satisfaction. As the difference between the roles of men and women is reduced, the value and charm of marriage as a combination of complementary qualities and responsibilities has dissipated.

Most of these underlying changes are inherent in the nature of modern societies. In some modern countries, these changes have already altered the prevalence and role of marriage.

One of the important features of marriage is the expectation by husband and wife that the marriage is permanent, that each can count on the other for the rest of their lives. That expectation of permanence profoundly influences the whole relationship. Certainly in the United States, and in some other modern countries, the expectation of permanence has already been greatly eroded, and it will diminish more in the future.

Of course, the laws and pressures aimed at making marriage permanent, largely by making it difficult to dissolve, have harmed some people. Some marriages shouldn't be permanent. There are many bad things that result from marriages being held together by external forces. Each degree of external resistance to ending marriage, from very easy to almost impossible, has its own mix of benefits and costs.

The subject is immensely complicated and modern conditions have not existed long enough to provide reliable answers from experience. It seems clear, however, that modernity threatens the institution of marriage, though we don't know yet whether modern societies will find new ways to sustain marriage. What we already see in the United States is that long-term monogamy is less common than it used to be, but that it is still central to the society. Many people still marry and stay married. A good share of children are raised by their parents. In no way can one say that marriage has largely disappeared or stopped being a major part of American life. Marriage is still a serious option for young people, even though it is not the same kind of marriage that existed before the United States became a fully modern country, and not as many people expect to be married through most of their lives.

The potential future problem is the possibility that the role of marriage will pass some tipping point and then lose its important place in modern countries, or that it will have so little support, and be so uncommon, that it cannot provide the benefits to society that it has in the past. As a result, children may become less healthy psychologically, less inclined to engage in positive relationships with other people. It is not unreasonable to think that the result would be a harsher and less-civilized society.

Furthermore, the weakness of marriage may aggravate the tendency not to have children. If people are not "automatically" getting married, and marriage is regarded as the most appropriate setting for having children, the need to marry would be an additional inhibition against a decision to have children.

This brings us to the demographic problem the modern world will face. The evidence so far (with the exception of the United States) suggests that modern peoples will not have enough children to replace themselves. If future science continually extends the human life span, so that people keep living longer and longer, population will not fall even if women on average have fewer children than are necessary to replace the current population. However, once length of life stops increasing, regardless of whether people live five hundred or a thousand years, population will start to fall if on average each woman has fewer than about 2.1 children. Will the human race, at that point, begin a long decline toward extinction?

On the other hand, if life extension allows women to have children through a large part of their extended lives, perhaps more women would eventually have enough children to replace themselves.

The demographic future, it seems, offers two possibilities: Either we face the prospect of a much less populated planet, with the danger that the human race may die out, or human life may be extended by genetic manipulation beyond what we can imagine. If the latter, will humans disappear because we change ourselves into something different? People whose genes have been altered so that their normal life span is five hundred years may or may not be able to mate with the humans of today. If not, they would by definition be a different species, created by a deliberate form of evolution. But even if such life-extended people were technically the same species as we are, they would be fundamentally different from us. Would we have preserved our kind if we transform ourselves into a species that live five hundred or a thousand years? Does it make any difference whether the transition is so quick that people with a five-hundred-year life span live alongside people like us, rather than, say, a fifty-year increase in life span every century?

There is no point in trying to evaluate the scientific issues regarding the possibility of such an extension of life, about which there is serious disagreement. It can't be done by eliminating diseases, that is, by curing or preventing cancer or heart disease. It can only be done by slowing or delaying the aging of all of our essential organ systems. Nobody knows yet whether the critical aging in all organs is the result of a single process, or whether the aging of each organ is a separate process that would have to be modified separately. Today, the possibility is an open question, an immeasurable opportunity or danger that can only be considered hypothetically.

Long life extension is perhaps the extreme example of a broad category of potential choices that future science may provide to the modern world. The amount of scientific work in the next century alone will dwarf all the science done up to now. The number of scientists, and the amount of money spent on scientific research, is increasing rapidly. The tools available to scientists are also continually improving. While the mountain of biological research in recent years has made scientists aware of how much they don't know about the human body, especially the human brain, it has also created much knowledge that the enlarged scientific enterprise of the future can build upon. Whether or not we will ever be able to modify our genes substantially to slow aging and extend lifespan, there can be little doubt that one effect of modern wealth and knowledge will be the development of many ways to artificially "improve" the human body and mind.

Of course, new measures to improve human abilities will raise safety issues, and there will be tradeoffs in which gains are counterbalanced by losses or risks (consider the widespread use of steroids in competitive athletics). But those questions are not the major problem for the modern world. The big problem is that we may not know who we are. Suppose we learned that porpoises are even smarter and more capable than we thought, and we developed a way to change ourselves into porpoises, and thus could have lives that are better in every measurable way, while doing less damage to the environment. Would this be a triumph? Would it be a success for science and modernity? Most people would not want their grandchildren to be porpoises, however happy, healthy, and environmentally beneficial such a conversion would be. We want humans to have better lives and to continue to be human. So we have to ask how much we can "improve" ourselves and still be ourselves.

One perspective on this question of how much change is compatible with what we are is the change that modernity has already made. We have already shown that, for the mass of people, modern societies, and the lives of people who live in them, are crucially different from all previous societies. While we have not yet changed life span significantly, we have certainly multiplied life expectancy, which is what most people feel. Modernity has already changed the lives of most people in modern countries—even their bodies and perhaps their minds are changed. Yet we certainly don't feel that we are becoming a different species. We feel strongly that we share our humanity with the earliest modern humans—the Cro-Magnon paintings in the caves of Lascaux or Altamira, for example, speak to us across tens of thousands of years. Presumably, therefore, we could make comparable further changes without beginning to feel separated from our ancestors.

Wherever one wants to put the line, it seems virtually certain that science and technology will in some approaching century give us the power to do things that will change humans into something essentially different from what we are now. Perhaps it will be by greatly postponing aging, perhaps by combining the human brain with computer networks in ways that make it unclear who is controlling whom.

The possibility of new ability to change human qualities is a problem for the modern world in two ways. First, it will have to face dilemmas and make decisions that people never had to make before about the fundamental features or character of our species and how much we want to preserve these essential characteristics. Second, we are likely to have to live through transition periods in which only a few people have the ability to, or choose to, use new powers, and the world is divided between those who have "moved on" and those who are still familiar kinds of human beings.

A common assumption is that modernity drives out religion. As people come to know scientific reality and true history, this thinking goes, they will stop relying on the myths of religion. As people become more sophisticated and more able to control their lives, they will no longer feel the need to believe in or rely on some kind of God. Modern people, it is said, don't need God; they are too aware of evolution to be able to believe in an all-powerful creator, and they are aware that religion has been a major cause of war.

So far this assumption has not been borne out by events. While it is true that many modern people are not religious, and religion has become a weaker force in some modern parts of the world, it is also true that many modern people are religious. Not only is the United States, the quintessential modern country, one of the most religious countries in the world, but in countries like Korea, the Philippines, and others, religious people are one of the leading sectors of the population. As I wrote some time ago, "secularism is only the first, innocent, response to modernity."

Although we cannot yet predict how religion will fare in the future, we should note that religion is potentially relevant to some of the great problems of the modern world. For example, as an arena in which people commonly face issues beyond themselves, establish their relationship to the mysteries of life, and try to serve a higher authority, religion may be a source of answers to the question, "What is the essential nature of human beings, and is it right for us to change it?" Indeed, for many people religion is a source of meaning and purpose in their lives. If people no longer find meaning and purpose in fighting poverty, tyranny, and war, because those have become yesterday's problems, some may turn to religious sources of meaning and purpose.

Some argue that one of the factors preventing modern politics from being more successful is that so many people seek personal redemption through their political life. This is bad for politics and is probably a poor way to achieve redemption. Perhaps, the more religion moves people, and provides a source of redemption, fewer people will enter politics to redeem their souls, and then politics might become more effective as it struggles with the practical decisions of a changing and increasingly complex world.

Religion may also be something that helps people become able to compensate for the loss of traditions and relationships and other emotionally sustaining features of life that are undercut by the change and competition and pursuit of efficiency of modernity. Modernity creates human needs that some people can fulfill through religion. If religion becomes the last or major social support for marriage, for example, its importance may be increased for those who feel strongly about the value of marriage.

Of course religion, when it is defined as a belief or faith in some kind of God, is not just something that can be picked up like a tool.

It is based on the truth of God, which is not known. It seems likely that, as science and understanding increases, many people will conclude that there is no God and that many others will come to believe that there is a God whose existence and will has implications for human life.

My conclusion is that, however successful we are at eliminating poverty, tyranny, and war, we are not going to run out of problems. Moving to a new history means moving to a new set of threats to human welfare and happiness, new threats that are at least as profound and dangerous as the familiar threats of the past. By showing what history tells us we can expect from the modern future, I hope this book will encourage people to begin to worry about these real challenges and recognize how many of today's problems are on the path to becoming part of history. Since we have at least a century of transition left to get through, I hope this broad perspective of what is happening in history—the unique passage from traditional to modern—will improve our ability to act wisely in our current changing world.

NOTE

1. This discussion of the family, it should be emphasized, has nothing to do with the contemporary debates about individual rights and of the role of homosexuals. My description of traditional marriage is not an argument that other kinds of marriages are somehow improper. The generalizations used here do not contradict the fact that there are many exceptions, nor do they imply that minorities should be suppressed or discriminated against. Nor do all people have to act in the way that usually is best for children.

NOTE ON THE RELATIONSHIP OF THE IDEAS OF HERMAN KAHN TO THIS BOOK

I was twenty-eight when I first met Herman Kahn. In the summer of 1960, I was asked to participate in and prepare a summary of a "peace game" that he and Don Brennan were leading at Massachusetts Institute of Technology's Endicott House. That fall I went to work for him at RAND, and when Herman left RAND to start Hudson Institute the following summer, I became his junior partner, working with him on both management and research.

Herman was my friend and mentor for over twenty years. He was a fascinating and brilliant teacher, with many kinds of wisdom to impart to the young lawyer that I was when we started. We worked together daily for the next twelve years, and now I cannot untangle what part of my thinking is my own from what I learned from Herman. Undoubtedly, he was the leader and principal source of ideas, but perhaps in a few cases I helped him develop the ideas we came to share.

This book has two main themes. The first is the understanding of our time as an era in which the world is in the middle of changing from the way it always was to a time of wealth. Herman developed this theme in great depth in his book *World Economic Development: 1979 and Beyond* (Westview Press, 1979), using the phrase "the great transition" to summarize the concept. I used a parallel phrase, *Passage to a Human World*, as the title of a book I wrote eight years later. But my thinking about this goes back to the time at Hudson Institute when Herman was working out these ideas, partly in discussions with me and other members of the Hudson research staff.

Now, with thirty more years of history behind us, I here develop this conception of where we are in very long-term history, including the future, somewhat more explicitly than Herman did. The basic idea, however, is the same one we talked about and wrote about earlier. To some extent, the idea of a "great transition" to modernity is so obvious that no one can claim authorship. Even so, despite Herman's large efforts and my smaller efforts over many years to spread the idea, it still seems controversial to most people.

Herman devoted great attention to the resistance to modernization, and to some of the philosophical questions it raises, which I mention generally but do not elaborate on. This book pays more attention to the historical structure of the transition and the definition of modernity.

The second theme in this book is the definition of a "war system," which has existed as long as there have been nations, and my assertion that in any region where all countries are modern countries, as I define "modern," there will be no war system. In other words, I am saying that in the modern world that is coming there will be no war system—and very little, if any, war. While this theme is compatible with Herman's thinking, it is not a set of ideas that he developed or presented.

A third key element of this book is based on the work that Herman led at Hudson, where my thinking was first formed. This element is the confident rejection of the Club of Rome and other Malthusians who assert that shortages of raw materials, and more pollution than can be handled, doom expectations of a prosperous world in the future. This doomsday perspective was reflected in the Carter administration's *Global 2,000* Report (Council of Environmental Quality and Department of State, 2000). During the time I was at Hudson, Herman became a leading voice—often in partnership with Julian Simon—exposing the error of this point of view (see Paul Dragos Aligica, *Prophecies of Doom and Scenarios of Progress* [Continuum, 2007].)

I absorbed the ideas about why Malthusianism should be rejected as these ideas were developed, learning much from Herman. My original form of presenting the argument was a major component of *Passage*, but very few pages here are devoted to the subject, which has been covered in a variety of books and articles in the last thirty years.

In brief, except for the idea that the war system is incompatible with modern countries, the main ideas here are ideas that are also in Herman Kahn's work and that I originally learned from or with him.

BIBLIOGRAPHICAL COMMENTS

Most of the vast literature on economic development concerns special problems regarding capital, culture, the role of middle class, timing, aid policies, and so on. There is relatively little debate about the main proposition guiding this book, that (1) economic development—modernization—is natural and "easy" and to be expected in any country that achieves minimum adequate government, and (2) therefore most or all countries should be expected to become modern.

The economic and other relevant literature is well reported in David Weil's outstanding textbook *Economic Growth*, 2nd ed. (Addison Wesley, 2008).

Lectures on Economic Growth, by Robert Lucas, Jr. (Harvard, 2002), uses theoretical economic analysis to understand the observed realities of differential economic growth throughout the world.

David S. Landes's *The Wealth and Poverty of Nations: Why Some Are So Rich and Others So Poor* (W.W. Norton, 1998) is a classic discussion of why economic growth has happened in some countries before other countries. His argument, at least by implication, supports the idea that economic growth can be achieved anywhere that it is not throttled by government greed or foolishness.

The best overall source for historical data and perspective related to economic growth is Angus Maddison, *Contours of the World*

Economy 1-2030 AD: Essays in Macro-Economic History (Oxford University, 2007).

Herman Kahn's main book on this subject is *World Economic Development: 1979 and Beyond* (Morrow Quill Paperbacks, 1979). It discusses extensively all the anti-growth arguments and feelings.

Probably the best population projections for 2100 are those of the International Institute for Applied Systems Analysis (IIASA) in Vienna (see Wolfgang Lutz, Warren Sanderson, and Sergei Scherbov, *IIASA's 2007 Probabilistic World Population Projections*, IIASA World Population Program Online Data Base of Results 2008 [www.iiasa.ac.at]).

A good comparative discussion of various sources of long-term population projections and of the issues involved in making such projections can be found in Brian C. O'Neill, Deborah Balk, Melanie Brickman, and Markos Ezra, "A Guide to Global Population Projections," *Demographic Research* 4, 203–88 (2001).

A good summary of the question of what recent demographic experience may be showing about human aging and changing life span is provided by James W. Vaupel, "Biodemography of Human Ageing," *Nature* 464, 536–42 (2010).

Julian Simon's *The Theory of Population and Economic Growth* (Blackwell, 1986) is just what the title says it is. His updated *The Ultimate Resource 2* (Princeton, 1996) provides theory and data to understand why the population growth now expected does not doom the world to shortages of natural resources or to unmanageable pollution problems. Julian Simon and Herman Kahn, eds., *The Resourceful Earth: A Response to Global 2000 (Report to the President)* (Blackwell, 1984), contains chapters on each fundamental resource—such as food, forests, water, minerals, and so forth—showing how detached from reality were the predictions presented by the Carter administration's report.

In my *Passage to a Human World: The Dynamics of Creating Global Wealth* (Transaction Publishers, 1988), I provide non-technical arguments to explain why we need not expect to run out of the raw materials we need or to have pollution problems we cannot handle.

The most important confirmation of the connection between postindustrial (or information) economies and the character and behavior of countries is presented in Ronald Inglehart and Christian Welzel, *Modernization, Cultural Change, and Democracy: The Human Development Sequence* (Oxford, 2005). The authors use a large body of data from many years of international surveys of values to demonstrate that as countries become more advanced in socio-economic terms, their citizens' values change, eventually becoming self-expression values that produce effective liberal democracy. The book is an extraordinary achievement—the best kind of academic study—and the culmination of an immense amount of work over many years.

Learned Hand was a lawyer and an outstanding judge, not a political scientist, but his speech "Democracy: Its Presumptions and Realities" is one of the most thoughtful and creative discussions ever written of how American democracy actually works and the values it provides. It can be found in Irving Dilliard, ed., *The Spirit of Liberty: Papers and Addresses of Learned Hand* (Vintage Books, 1959).

The argument for the value of nation-states in protecting human rights and preserving healthy democracy is found in Natan Sharansky (with Shira Wolosky Weiss), *Defending Identity: Its Indispensable Role in Protecting Democracy* (Public Affairs, 2008).

When I started writing this book, I expected to argue that when all countries are modern democracies, wars would be rare or non-existent because democracies don't go to war with each other. But I came to realize that the lack of war in an all-modern world has a much deeper basis than the reluctance of democracies to fight one another. The end of the war system, as described in chapter 4, is a more basic reason that war will not be an important part of modern life when the transition to a modern world is completed. Nonetheless, the historic evidence about the unwillingness of democracies to go to war with other democracies continues to be of interest, partly because this unwillingness works even today, before all the world is modern. This historic evidence is presented in Spencer Weart, *Never at War: Why Democracies Will Not Fight One Another* (Yale University Press, 1998).

The preeminent scholar of the history of the Middle East and of Islam is Bernard Lewis, Cleveland Dodge Professor Emeritus at Princeton University and the Princeton Institute of Advanced Study. The following are among his books bearing on the discussion of the Islam in this book: Bernard Lewis and Buntzie Churchill, *Islam: The Religion and the People* (Wharton School Publishing, 2008); Bernard Lewis, *The Crisis of Islam: Holy War and Unholy Terror* (Modern Library, 2003); and Bernard Lewis, *Islam and the West* (Oxford University Press, 1993). There are eminent scholars of Islam who privately criticize Lewis and other students of Islam for being unwilling to give publicly their real assessments of Islam for fear of criticism or retribution. It is certainly a field requiring care to avoid diplomatic landmines. Lewis has also been widely criticized—essentially rejected—by Edward Said and his many followers in the field of Middle East studies. However, these criticisms do not stand up to a reading of Lewis's work and can safely be ignored by anyone seeking to understand Islam and the Middle East.

The great contemporary source for trying to understand modern Islam is MEMRI (Middle East Media Research Institute), which daily translates and posts on the Internet (MEMRI.org) extensive selections from the Muslim press, speeches, and documents in English and other languages so that readers can learn for themselves about contemporary Islam in its own words.

Leon Kass, *Life, Liberty, and the Defense of Dignity: The Challenge for Bioethics* (Encounter, 2002), presents the principles with which Professor Kass, who is a medical doctor and a Ph.D. in biochemistry, approaches the challenges that modern science is bringing to humanity. Although Kass is often referred to as a "bioethicist," he calls himself a "humanist."

INDEX